ERASE THE PATRIARCHY

AN ANTHOLOGY OF ERASURE POETRY

EDITED BY ISOBEL O'HARE

This book is published by University of Hell Press

www.universityofhellpress.com

Cover and Interior Design by Olivia Croom Hammerman
oliviacroomdesign.com

Handwriting Font by Greg Gerding

Published in the United States of America

ISBN 978-1-938753-37-4

CONTENTS

JOURNALISM & MEDIA

"build new men and burn the old ones down"

RELIGION

"the foulest abominations"

SCIENCE & EDUCATION

"the guilt that men deny"

MUSIC

"I just wanna con u"

HOLLYWOOD

"The fact is I am a predator"

SPORTS

"I had an unfair advantage"

LITERATURE

"fuck tender beauty"

INTRODUCTION

THE IDEA FOR *Erase the Patriarchy* was born out of my own book, *all this can be yours,* published by University of Hell Press in 2018. That project, which takes the apology statements of famous men accused of sexual assault and redacts them down to pithy statements such as "My dick is a question I run from" and "I came of age in a culture of demons I respect more than women," went viral in the midst of the #MeToo moment near the end of 2017. At the peak of that experience, my Twitter account received half a million views in a 24-hour period and suddenly people like Judd Apatow and Saul Williams were following me. My cell phone, which had social media notifications enabled at that time, did not have a black screen for a single second during those 24 hours, lighting up constantly with new tweets, retweets, and suggestions that I kill myself or at the very least stop demonizing the poor men who had been victimized by "false accusations."

One of the best outcomes of the project for me was witnessing other people respond to it with their own erasures. People sent me, in Facebook comments and private messages, their own redactions of the same apologies as well as other statements and documents made by powerful men. In Facebook threads where men argued against #MeToo, my friends took screenshots of their comments and redacted them, reposting the redacted statements as clever retorts. A commenter who criticized my work in a thread at *AV Club* received a redacted version of his comment from another commenter. I started to imagine these redactions as a new form of conversational protest, the selective editing of the words of men in power to reveal their deceptions and reflect them back, a sort of reverse funhouse mirror of words where the distortion is more truthful than the original statement.

Because the act of redaction had been so cathartic for me, and because so many people expressed interest in joining in, I came up with the idea for an anthology of erasure poems aimed at redacting patriarchal history to point out its misuses and abuses of power, its prejudices, its violence, and how it pits us against one another. It has been an absolute pleasure and a wonder to read and consider all of the submissions sent our way, and I only wish we could have published all of them.

One of my concerns during the 2017 #MeToo moment was its focus on the experiences of predominantly prominent white women in a lucrative industry in the United States. There didn't seem to be enough of an emphasis on the experiences of society's most marginalized individuals across the spectrums of race, class, sexuality, and gender. Witnessing #MeToo from within the United States made me curious about the moment's manifestation in other countries, and I was pleased to receive a number of submissions from outside the US that respond to political and systemic injustices happening around the globe. In these pages, you'll find works from people living in various countries as well as many Americans working from dual identities across multiple nations of origin.

As in *all this can be yours*, statements in *Erase the Patriarchy* are organized into themed categories connected to different aspects of the cultural conversation. Those sections are as follows:

Government | "I am a man who has history"
Journalism & Media | "build new men and burn the old ones down"
Religion | "the foulest abominations"
Science & Education | "the guilt that men deny"
Music | "I just wanna con u"
Hollywood | "The fact is I am a predator"
Sports | "I had an unfair advantage"
Literature | "fuck tender beauty"

In these erasures, you will find critiques of anti-immigration policies; statements made against queer and disabled people; antisemitism; nations founded on inequality; song lyrics, poems, and novels that celebrate the oppression of women; seminal scientific documents steeped in misogyny; entitled attitudes toward lucrative prizes; exclusionary hiring practices in male-dominated industries; and more.

A big part of this moment has been us reckoning with our own history and confronting not only the biases and prejudices that we were raised with but also those of our heroes. We've had to admit to ourselves that some of the people we grew up idolizing have held deeply troubling views and have caused harm to the vulnerable. As contributor Addie Tsai notes in their process statement, "It's hard to break up with your idols."

It has often felt like this project could continue forever.

As I fielded submissions, the Brett Kavanaugh hearings were taking place and Christine Blasey Ford's testimony spurred a renewal of the #MeToo moment with the hashtag #WhyIDidntReport, which had sexual assault survivors flooding Twitter with their stories of systemic sexism and victim-blaming that keeps survivors from risking reputation, dignity, and career by reporting their assaults.

While putting the collection together, Jeffrey Epstein died in jail as he awaited trial for the sex trafficking of children.

At the time of writing this introduction, Joe Biden, himself accused of sexual assault, is the last man standing in a campaign season that carried Democrats from #MeToo to #BlueNoMatterWho, a journey that makes little sense if the rallying cry to "Believe Women" or "Believe Survivors" carried any weight beyond what is considered politically expedient. Any woman hoping to become Biden's running mate will be put in the impossible position of denying his accuser's claims and standing by him to the end, yet another confirmation that politics and presidents will always be seen as more important than survivors. And the COVID-19 pandemic has provided the latest round of excuses as to why survivors of injustice must continue to wait for their voices to be heard. There is always some catastrophic occurrence, some crisis ever more urgent that beckons our attention away from those crying out.

When will we learn that what is good for the marginalized is also what is good for the earth, for all of us?

Perhaps by the time of publication, a miracle will have occurred. The Democratic Party will have replaced Biden with another candidate, someone who cares about the most marginalized people in our society, who prioritizes the environment at a time of global climate crisis, and has no history of abuse toward anyone. Or maybe Biden will admit to past wrongdoing, making moves toward personal accountability and restitution. By the time this book goes to print, more will undoubtedly be known about the details of his accuser's case, and while I don't have much faith that either of the fantasies I've laid out here will come to fruition, at least we'll continue to have the tools of erasure at our disposal.

We are still very much in the early stages of a widespread societal understanding of the psychology behind trauma, and projects like this one aim to aid in that understanding. By exposing not only the abuses themselves but also popular myths around the "perfect victim" or the "right" way to respond to assault, racism, homophobia, or any other act of hatred and intolerance, these erasures contribute to an enduring conversation aimed at the liberation of all marginalized people from all forms of oppression. This collection is but a small piece of that conversation. If you'd like to explore more erasures of a sociopolitical/historical nature, please refer to the Suggested Reading List at the back of the book.

ISOBEL O'HARE
MAY 2020

GOVERNMENT

"I am a man
who has history"

in the history of this country

men abuse

women

I am

a man who has history

I live in Minnesota, and I voted for Al Franken in 2008, and again in 2014. But in the fall of 2017 when accusations of sexual misconduct started piling up, I joined the calls for him to resign. I watched his resignation speech live, so hopeful that he would use that moment to speak important and difficult truths about patriarchy, about systemic violence against women, about his own complicity. I was disappointed.

Since I didn't hear what I was hoping for in Franken's speech, I started working on erasures to show the kinds of statements I believe he should have made. I erased the justifications, the arrogant self-defense, the arguing, the posturing, and I left only straightforward truths.

Writing has always been a way for me to understand and cope with the world around me, but this is my first attempt at erasure poetry. The process of choosing from and combining words already on the page proved both grounding and intensely creative, a concrete manifestation of what I have always believed to be true when I write—the words are already there; my task is to find them. In this case, when I found them, I rubbed crayon over them and erased the rest into the background with watercolors. Incorporating visual art with written art was also a first for me, and it proved to be a gratifying new way to find and see my own words, and my own truth.

JODI VERSAW

Listen

JUDGE BRETT M. KAVANAUGH:

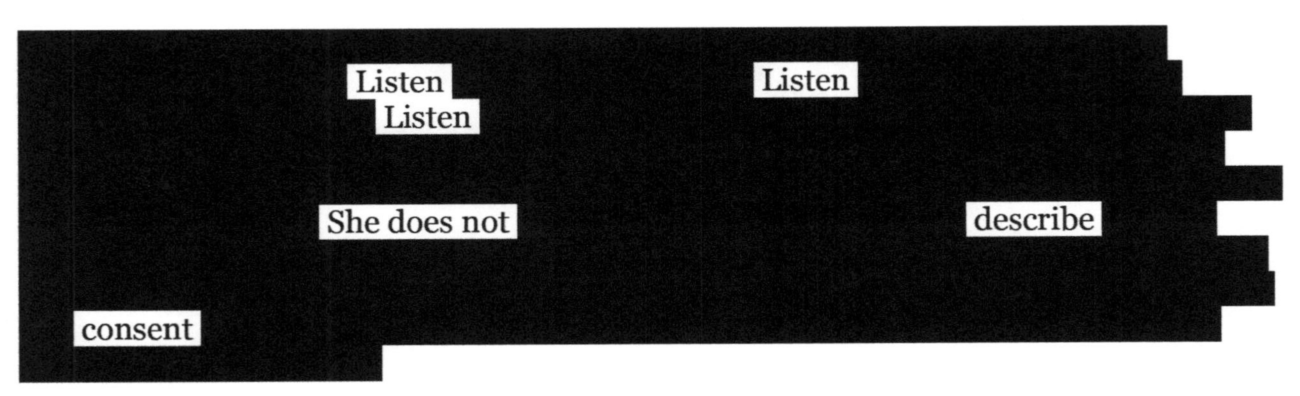

Listen
Listen
Listen
She does not
describe
consent

The source text for this erasure poem is the transcript of Brett Kavanaugh's opening statement to the Senate Judiciary Committee, published on September 26, 2018, in *The New York Times*. The presentation of the erasure, with language blacked out and removed, is meant to resemble a highly redacted government document. The process of redaction is sometimes referred to as "sanitization," a term which feels fitting, considering the foul tone of Kavanaugh's speech, the stench that still echoes in my ears.

As I listened to Kavanaugh's testimony, I was struck by the irony of his insistence on being heard—reflected not only in the aggressive volume of his voice, but also in his repeated command for us to *listen*—as if he were the one who had to endure years of silence, as if his voice was the one silenced and ignored. I wanted to drown him out, to argue against him, to bring Christine Blasey Ford's account and experience to the forefront. I wanted her truth, the truth, our truths, to be heard.

AMY ASH

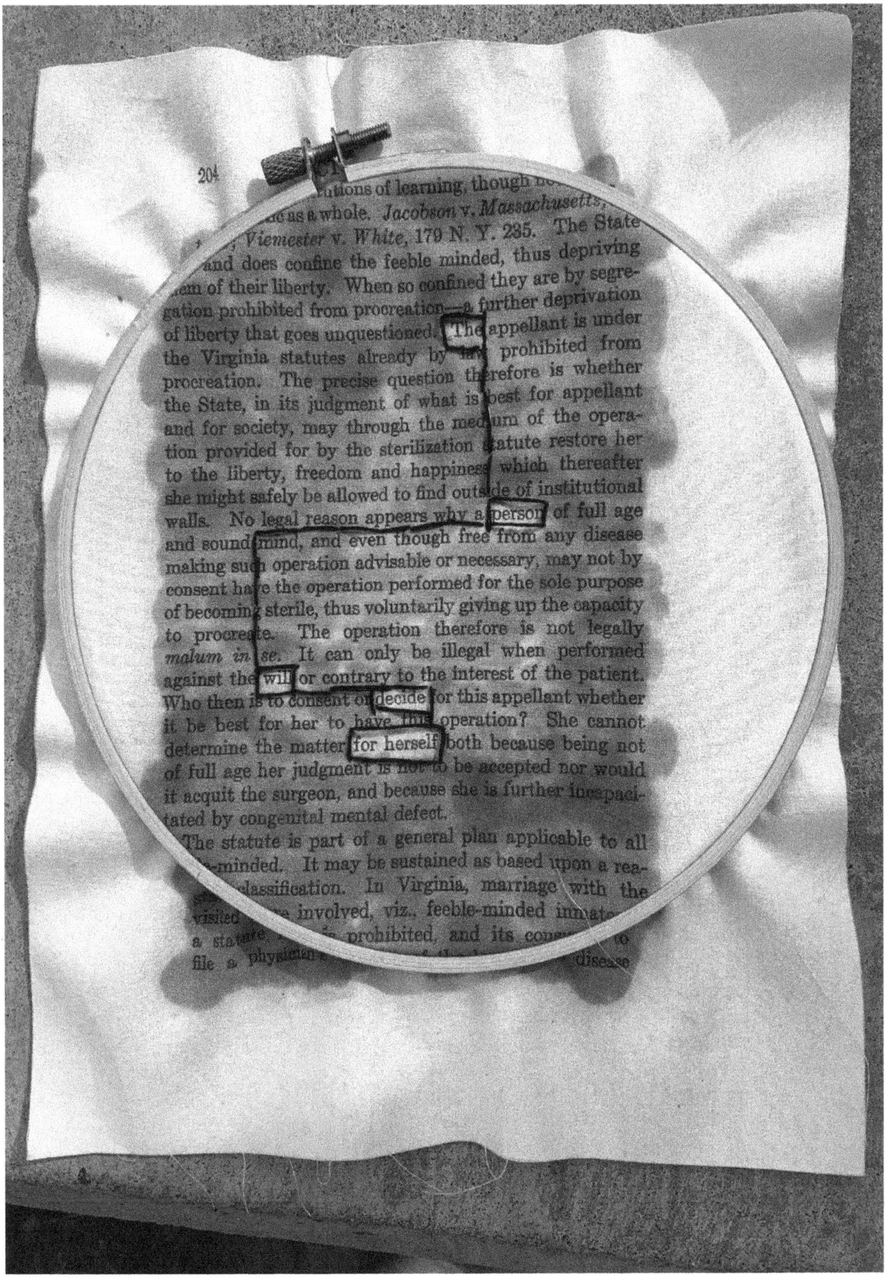

…itutions of learning, though … lic as a whole. *Jacobson* v. *Massachusetts*, … *Viemester* v. *White*, 179 N. Y. 235. The State … and does confine the feeble minded, thus depriving …em of their liberty. When so confined they are by segregation prohibited from procreation—a further deprivation of liberty that goes unquestioned. The appellant is under the Virginia statutes already by law prohibited from procreation. The precise question therefore is whether the State, in its judgment of what is best for appellant and for society, may through the medium of the operation provided for by the sterilization statute restore her to the liberty, freedom and happiness which thereafter she might safely be allowed to find outside of institutional walls. No legal reason appears why a person of full age and sound mind, and even though free from any disease making such operation advisable or necessary, may not by consent have the operation performed for the sole purpose of becoming sterile, thus voluntarily giving up the capacity to procreate. The operation therefore is not legally *malum in se.* It can only be illegal when performed against the will or contrary to the interest of the patient. Who then is to consent or decide for this appellant whether it be best for her to have this operation? She cannot determine the matter for herself both because being not of full age her judgment is not to be accepted nor would it acquit the surgeon, and because she is further incapacitated by congenital mental defect.

The statute is part of a general plan applicable to all …-minded. It may be sustained as based upon a rea… classification. In Virginia, marriage with the … involved, viz., feeble-minded inmat… a statute … prohibited, and its cons… file a physician… disease

The piece I made is an erasure from a page of the Supreme Court's 1927 decision in *Buck vs. Bell*, in which Oliver Wendell Holmes, delivering the decision of the Court, declared that forcibly sterilizing a disabled woman was not a violation of her Constitutional rights. This decision has never been overturned.

To complete my erasure, I printed the document on cotton and blacked out the words using iodine tincture of the sort one might use to sterilize an area before a surgery. Then, I framed the erasure in an embroidery hoop to signal the piece's transition from its original textual form to a new object—also its move from a traditionally male realm (sadly, the Supreme Court) to a traditionally female realm. Embroidery hoops of this kind have long been used in embroidery and needlepoint—the kind of piecework that it's easy to imagine Carrie Buck (and other nameless women) doing as they passed the years in the Virginia State Colony for Epileptics and Feebleminded. The black stitching was used to evoke both needlepoint and sutures.

In its new incarnation, the document says simply, "The person will decide for herself"—a refrain with perpetual (and renewed) urgency, as the reproductive rights of women are under assault. (Using the pronoun "herself" with the antecedent "person" is deliberate, and a violation of the traditional laws of grammar.) Now, as in Carrie Buck's time, the reproductive rights and bodily agency of disabled women are particularly vulnerable. I identify as a disabled woman, so this issue is especially important for me.

ANDREA AVERY

Attorney General Sessions Delivers Remarks on DACA
Washington, DC
~
Tuesday, September 5, 2017
Remarks as prepared for delivery

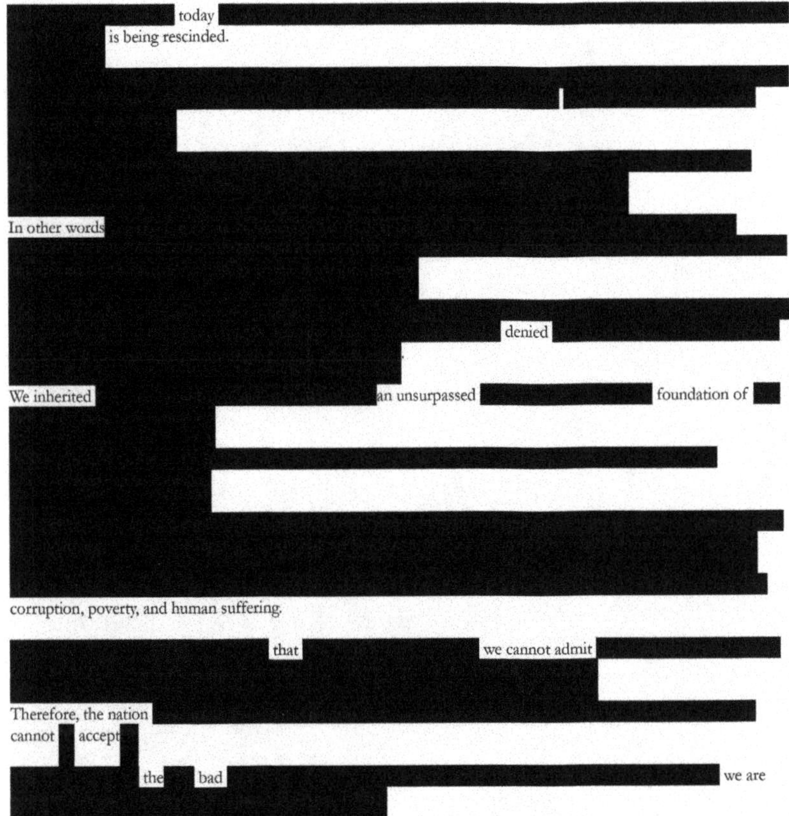

today
is being rescinded.

In other words

denied

We inherited an unsurpassed foundation of

corruption, poverty, and human suffering.

that we cannot admit

Therefore, the nation
cannot accept

the bad we are

Betsy DeVos, Title IX, and the "Both Sides" Approach to Sexual Assault

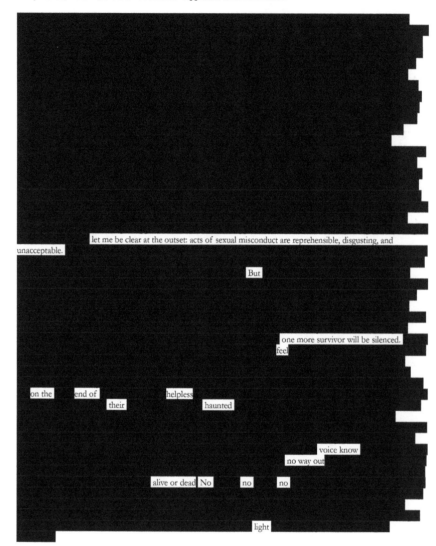

The texts I'd chosen were Attorney General Session's remarks with the decision to rescind DACA, and Secretary of Education, Betsy DeVos' Title IX, "Both Sides" Approach to Sexual Assault speech.

The leader of the current administration obfuscates the truth while his cronies unctuously clean up 45's clearly sexist, xenophobic, and racist positions. The reality of their character simmers just below their grins and populist posturing. Who they are exists in what they say, and I wanted to draw that forth in both of my erasure pieces.

For AG Session's speech, I found a tone of American guilt within the words, the idea that American pride largely rests on American denial. Nationalism no longer rests in our pride for who we are, or our will to be better. But rather, a lie, a jingoism is protected at all costs because facing it would destroy us.

For Betsy DeVos' speech, I wanted to capture the systemic issue of rape apology in the Secretary of Education's entire convoluted ramblings about equity, moral obligations, and fair justice. Initially, I wanted the piece to only be short, viewed mostly as blackened space. However, in reexamining the words, I had to draw greater attention to the Sisyphean drudge that survivors confront every time they seek justice and how the silence of trauma is a currency that America runs on. The system does not work for all people equally, but we cannot admit that. Or at least, those in power positions can't.

CHRISTOPHER MARTINEZ

YOUR FUTURE IS AT STAKE IN THIS ELECTION!!!!!!!!

People are well aware of Trump's shortcomings, but they are nothing compared to Hillary Clinton's total corruption, lies and felonies.

Trump wants to secure our borders against illegals pouring into our country and send these law breakers back where they belong. We will save billions in benefits to illegals. Trump will reduce business taxes and bring jobs back home. Tax revenues will increase and the budget deficit will decline. Trump wants to renegotiate trade deals and stop allowing China to manipulate trade and currency laws. Prohibition against immigrants with AIDS and STDs will be put back into place that were illegally removed by Obama. Trump will protect the Second Amendment and rebuild our military to defend against warmonger Putin. Donald Trump is the Common Sense candidate.

Hillary will allow millions of illegals to pour into our country, draining more resources from local, state and federal governments. More Americans will be murdered by illegals. Hillary's tax increases will drag the economy down. The national debt will continue to rise. Our military will continue to weaken while Russia grows ever more aggressive. Hillary gets her radical politicians onto the Supreme Court which then declares the Second Amendment does not allow for private ownership of guns. Fascist Clinton has promised to bypass Congress and use Executive Orders in violation of our Constitutional checks and balances put into place by the Founding Fathers. Hillary Clinton is the polarizing candidate and an extremist.

Never before has the news media been so blatantly one sided as they are in 2016. A report on Politico.com on Oct 25 showed a whopping 91 percent of news coverage about Donald Trump on the three broadcast nightly newscasts over the past 12 weeks were 'hostile'. **It's a sad day in America when we have to rely on hackers to give us the truth while the media works hard to hide it from us.**

over

<u>YOUR</u> FUTURE IS

over

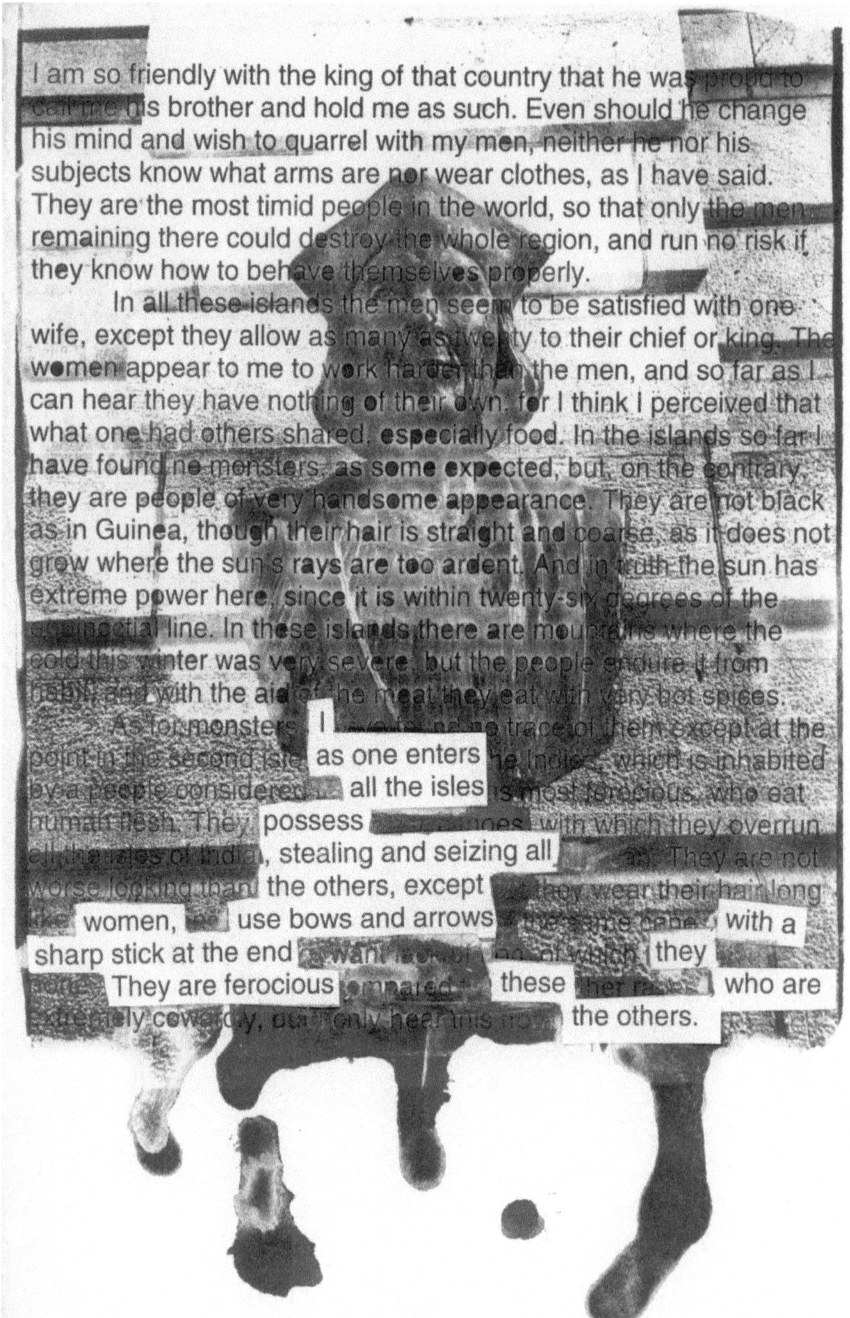

I am so friendly with the king of that country that he was proud to
call me his brother and hold me as such. Even should he change
his mind and wish to quarrel with my men, neither he nor his
subjects know what arms are nor wear clothes, as I have said.
They are the most timid people in the world, so that only the men
remaining there could destroy the whole region, and run no risk if
they know how to behave themselves properly.

In all these islands the men seem to be satisfied with one
wife, except they allow as many as twenty to their chief or king. The
women appear to me to work harder than the men, and so far as I
can hear they have nothing of their own, for I think I perceived that
what one had others shared, especially food. In the islands so far I
have found no monsters, as some expected, but, on the contrary,
they are people of very handsome appearance. They are not black
as in Guinea, though their hair is straight and coarse, as it does not
grow where the sun's rays are too ardent. And in truth the sun has
extreme power here, since it is within twenty-six degrees of the
equinoctial line. In these islands there are mountains where the
cold this winter was very severe, but the people endure it from
habit, and with the aid of the meat they eat with very hot spices.

As for monsters, I

as one enters

all the isles

possess

, stealing and seizing all

the others, except

women, use bows and arrows with a

sharp stick at the end they

They are ferocious these who are

the others.

"Your Future is Over" was created from a flyer handed to me outside of my local polling place on Election Day 2016. The caucasian man who gave it to me felt compelled by his personal politics to distribute these printouts; presumably he hoped to sway undecided voters. I barely scanned it, put it in my pocket, voted, and dismissively tossed the paper on the dining room table when I emptied my pockets that evening. Then the election results came in, and what I thought was impossible became reality. On November 9th, 2016, I sat down and made this erasure knowing that I wanted to start with the headline and end with the page direction at the bottom. What surprised me in the emotion of the moment was that despite all I could have done with the political ramblings in between, nothing felt more accurate than the end result. Blacking out words never felt as necessary as it did that afternoon when I removed his shoddy rhetoric and found what little language was left on the page spoke the message of that day succinctly.

"Bloody Columbus" uses an alternative process photographic print technique to graphically illustrate the guilt in which Christopher Columbus deserves to be draped. The image of his bust is presented in hand-applied dripping chemicals rendered blood red. The photo is printed over a translated page from the explorer's personal journals. This incriminating backdrop discusses the native people he encountered in crude terms. The erasure flips the script. The colonizer admits to seizing land. The "others," in the form of armed women, are described as ferocious and able to defend themselves.

Unfortunately, history shows that the native people suffer mass genocide and Columbus is given a national holiday in the US. To this day, the bust in the photograph is on display outside of the Lancaster County Courthouse thanks to the public defense of the statue by the Knights of Columbus, a religiously affiliated fraternal organization. Its removal has been hotly debated in city council. The bust is at times defaced by anonymous citizens, often covered with a ski mask or brown paper bag. Not every American, or Lancastrian for that matter, ignores the bloody legacy of Columbus.

CAITLIN M. DOWNS

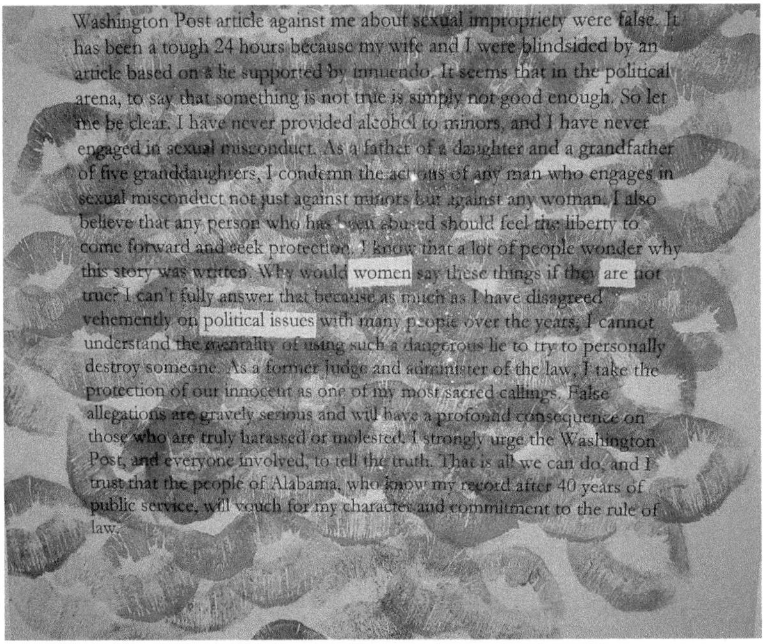

Washington Post article against me about sexual impropriety were false. It has been a tough 24 hours because my wife and I were blindsided by an article based on a lie supported by innuendo. It seems that in the political arena, to say that something is not true is simply not good enough. So let me be clear. I have never provided alcohol to minors, and I have never engaged in sexual misconduct. As a father of a daughter and a grandfather of five granddaughters, I condemn the actions of any man who engages in sexual misconduct not just against minors but against any woman. I also believe that any person who has been abused should feel the liberty to come forward and seek protection. I know that a lot of people wonder why this story was written. Why would women say these things if they are not true? I can't fully answer that because as much as I have disagreed vehemently on political issues with many people over the years, I cannot understand the mentality of using such a dangerous lie to try to personally destroy someone. As a former judge and administer of the law, I take the protection of our innocent as one of my most sacred callings. False allegations are gravely serious and will have a profound consequence on those who are truly harassed or molested. I strongly urge the Washington Post, and everyone involved, to tell the truth. That is all we can do, and I trust that the people of Alabama, who know my record after 40 years of public service, will vouch for my character and commitment to the rule of law.

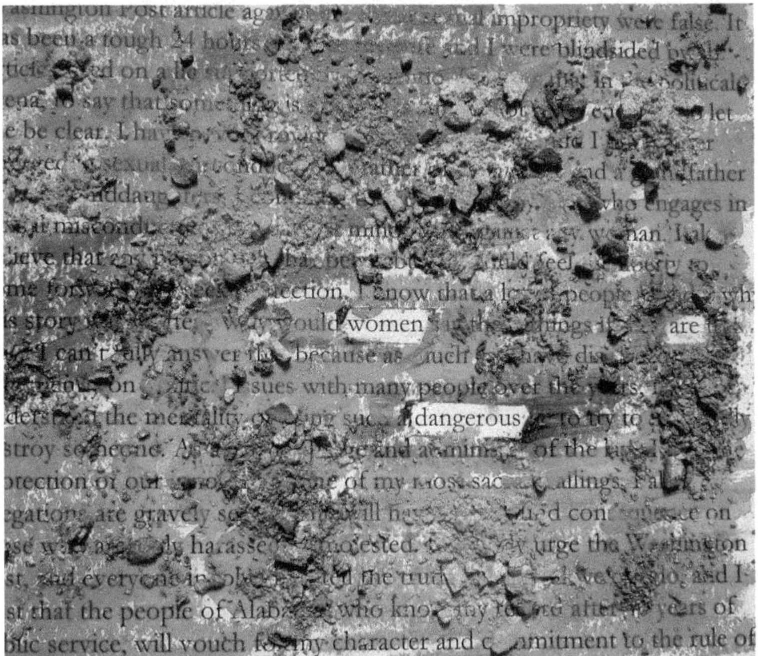

Washington Post article against me about sexual impropriety were false. It has been a tough 24 hours because my wife and I were blindsided by an

I condemn

any woman

who

will

tell the truth

The statement I've erased is one of many given by Roy Moore during the 2017 Alabama Special Election where he was running for Senate. Multiple women came forward with stories of Moore's prior sexual assault, and not only did Moore consistently deny any wrongdoing, he launched personal attacks on the victims, publicly vilifying and degrading them. This was all happening at the media height of the #MeToo movement, and it was a deeply upsetting moment for me on multiple fronts: as a woman, as a survivor of sexual assault, and as an Alabamian. I watched in horror while my home seemed to implode—so many people, even women and people I love, were willing to believe Moore over these women and vote for him, and it was a cruel reminder of why more women don't come forward about their abuse. Moore ended up losing the race, but by a margin that was disturbingly small. These erasures of his denials were my catharsis during those months—a means of un-twisting his words to get at the truth, and admittedly, a "fuck you" to Moore and men like him who abuse and expect the abused to stay silent.

RAYE HENDRIX

Reclamation

from Republican U.S. Senate Candidate Courtland Sykes'
2018 Statement about Women's Rights:

I want to come home to a home cooked dinner at six every night, one that
[Chanel, my fiancée] fixes and that I expect one day to have daughters learn to fix
after they become traditional homemakers and family wives.
Think Norman Rockwell here and Gloria Steinem be damned.
"I don't buy into radical **feminism's** crazed definition of
modern womanhood and I never did. They don't own that definition—
and never did. They made it up to suit their own nasty, snake-filled heads. …
And I don't buy the non-stop feminization campaign against manhood.
I don't **want** [daughters] to grow into **career** obsessed
banshees who forgo **home life and children**
and the **happiness of family** to become nail-biting
manophobic hell-bent feminist
she devils who **shriek from the tops of**
a thousand tall buildings…think they
could have **leap**ed **over in a single bound**
had men not been 'suppressing them.'
It's just nuts. It always **was.**
I support women's rights, but not **the** kind
that has oppressed natural womanhood for **five** long
decades—the kind **of** wrongheaded '**women**'s rights' **that**
allows mean-spirited radical feminists to use political correctness
and their little broom label of 'sexist' to **define** womanhood and women's **rights**
for me and my family,
for you and your family …
for my country and the world.
But there's good news. They're finished. Ask Hilary.
Someone should have **stood up**
and faced them off, **years ago.**"

The poem entitled "Reclamation" is an excerpt of Republican US Senate Candidate Courtland Sykes' 2018 statement about women's rights, which the candidate published widely. I have kept all of Sykes' words visible, but in faint gray, and have reclaimed a feminist manifesto in bold. I decided to let Sykes' content remain visible because I think that feminists must always keep such misogynistic ideology in our sights. Preserving the readability of his words reminds us of what we are up against. In my reclamation piece, Sykes' text recedes into the background. It is gray like ash, and from it a bold feminist statement rises.

DEBORAH FASS

Don J. Grundmann | NO PARTY PREFERENCE

A Campaign for

spiritual /sickness is

the way.

children are weapons to attack and destroy

children. i break

children so that current and future generations

will be manufactured into psychotics and destroyed.

n. Go Attack Children to join

this war/jihad against them.

59 Washington St. #152
Santa Clara, CA 95050

Tel: (510) 895-6789
E-mail: stoptheirs@hotmail.com
fight-the-power.org

My first approach was to nod, smile, and listen, and above all to be reasonable; to prove that I can at least do these things. After the General Public was reassured, I set to work.

It hurt in this boring and routine sort of way. I was, after all, casting my 2018 California midterm ballot. What I did with that Sharpie was essentially proofread, whittling down repetitive transphobic screed into condensed units of hatred, that I might lay bare the violent obsessions at work in the text.

It felt surgical and erotic. And dirty, too. Like something I should have been paid for.

IRIS MIRIAM BLOOMFIELD

Next Steps for FAMILIES

STEP 1
- You are
- the crime

STEP 2
- Within the next 48 hours, you will be violated
- your child will be a temporary child

STEP 3
How do I locate my child(ren)?

Action 1 - Call

Action 2 -
- the child's full name,
- 24 hours a day, 7 days a week, in Spanish or English.

Action 3 –

STEP 4
- After your court hearing, you will be red
- ICE will schedule your child(ren).
- ICE will provide access to legal self-help materials.

PASO 1

PASO 2

PASO 3

Asistencia para hablar en su idioma está disponible.

PASO 4

Inaugural Speech - Erasure

We
count and store our people.
we mine the world for ears

Every ear we gather

has special meaning. we are
transferring power
to

the wards of
cost. Wash
the
factories
, but not
the families

-- right now,

a red cross

is listening to

the movement of

children, safe or

trapped

in our rusted-out tombs

;

carnage

is The dream

of all Americans.

For many decades, we've enriched dust

;

we've defended the order to

decay.

We've made

the horizon

out

of ripped homes and

assembled

power.

From this moment on,

Every decision will be made

from the

ravages of

breath -- you

will never

build a bridge

of

hands .

We will follow two simple rules:

impose

the bedrock of our

minds

and

protect the

God

of

energies, industries and

technologies .

our souls

forget whether we are

blood

or a Flag.

we

ask the night sky

and

mountain and ocean to hear these words:

You will never ignore

our voice, our destiny.

We will make

wealth .

We will make America .

And yes, we will make God . And God bless America.

One of my favorite aspects of political erasure poetry has always been the ability to interact with something intentional. Politicians, leaders, and officials make thoughtless, reactionary comments every day, and the American news cycle eats it up with similarly inconsiderate and explosive coverage. But when something is *written down*, we pause. When a legislator pens an inflammatory tweet or a disastrous bill, we take notice of the weight and physicality of someone having to move the pen or type out the letters.

In my mind, this is where the true power of erasure poetry occurs: intentionally blacking out the text of someone, who was just as purposeful, in their own words. I approached the *Next Steps for Families* handout with this framework: a human wrote out these harsh and horrifying regulations separating parents from their children. I wanted to forcefully remind myself that this insulting document did not just shoot out of some impartial, government collective. These haphazard directions outline the improbable methods by which detained parents can even speak to their children, and someone's fingers were responsible for writing it.

Yes, this poem is a cry for awareness. Yes, this poem is my feeble attempt to strive for human rights and empathy. But even more so, I wrote this poem as conversation and condemnation, as dialogue with the person or persons who wrote *Next Steps for Families*. Too often,

I find myself more and more resigned to living under a government administration that is combative and powerful in the worst ways. Writing erasure poetry reminds me that politicians and leaders are not untouchable entities; they are fallible, they can be held personally responsible, and they are never above reproach. I hope that in some small way, this poem speaks back.

JERROD SCHWARZ

Donald J. Trump @realDonaldTrump · Jan 6
....Actually, throughout my life, my two greatest assets have been
lapdogs,
and
screaming

Inspired by Isobel O'Hare's erasure of sexual predator apologies, I began this meditation on the constant tweets from the president of the United States. If anyone ever needed to be edited, it was this person. To pore through his daily output, and construct some coherent message, was impossible. Instead, the totality becomes revelation and one becomes Andy from *The Shawshank Redemption* emerging from the sewer into a cleansing storm-shower. I recommend the exercise.

JOEL LARSON

I announce

a vessel

ready to transfer

the

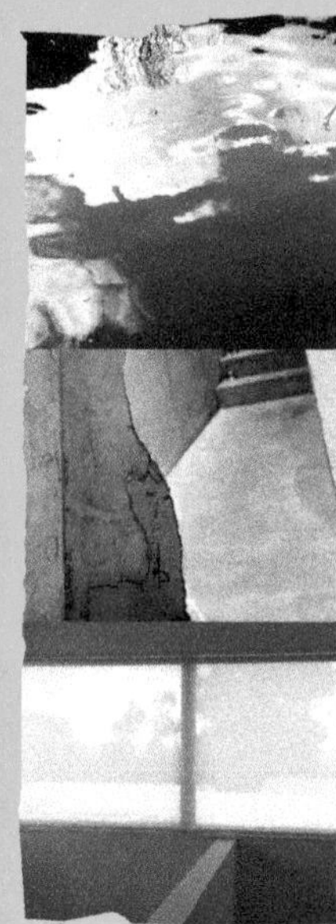

deep cooperation is that

the best welfare

The text I have selected is one of the early speeches our then prime minister of Australia John Howard made about the so-called "Pacific solution" that led to "off-shore processing" of refugees in the wake of the crisis surrounding the vessel the Tampa nearing the Australian shore. One of the things that people cite when they are criticised for xenophobic action is their fear for society, and women are often used as an example of people vulnerable if the "wrong sorts" enter our country—often ignoring what the real threats posed to women by systemic bias. By erasing Howard's speech (given at a press conference in Sydney on 2 September 2001, days before the world became yet more fearful) I wanted to find compassion within words that have haunted Australia's policies towards those less "lucky" than citizens of our so-called "lucky country." This compassion towards the less "lucky" is accompanied by images—collages and photographs—I have created that aim to turn upside down our sense of the pristine surface of Australian suburbia.

KATE MIDDLETON

But You Said You Would Knock Him Out, Mr President

I [redacted] condemn [redacted] gays and lesbians.

Jacob Zuma.

South Africa is known to have an exceptionally progressive constitution that protects all of its citizens. Our country has been shaped by a history of struggle and blood and all rights enshrined in our constitution have been hard earned. The queer in South Africa is protected by the constitution, but we are still persecuted in our lived realities regardless of race and class. It continues to be dangerous for us to even exist in our own country, a country that we fought to build and protect.

This has led to our queer community feeling disenfranchised and outright betrayed by the very institution we helped to build. A rising anger has been brewing in South Africa as queerphobia prevails despite our constitutional rights. This was made worse when rapist and former South African president, Jacob Zuma, made a careless comment about gay men in South African townships during South Africa's 2006 Heritage Day. The former president indicated that, in the townships, if one encounters a homosexual it is acceptable (perhaps even necessary) to knock them out to dismiss the queer's deviance from the bizarre heteronorms that dominate our society, and to assert one's masculinity in the face of someone who does not mirror it.

The former president then made a weakly apologetic statement to cover his tracks and to soothe the country's queer community. Naturally, we saw through this statement as it was evident that our own president had thrown us under the bus in the public sphere, spitting in the face of every queer person who fought during the struggle against Apartheid and any queer person who lives in fear in our townships.

My erasure poem is intended to return the favour.

By taking the former president's statement and erasing it, I am not allowing his queerphobia to be brushed under the rug. We have suffered too many indignities, and even writing this statement makes me seethe with a white-hot anger.

This erasure exposes the blatant queerphobia and toxic masculinity that South African politicians are allowed to perpetuate.

If we do not hold these powerful men accountable for their harmful statements and actions, they will continue to damage us.

KEGAN GASPAR

From the Debate in British Parliament on the 'Conciliation' Bill, to enfranchise about 1 million Women voters, 28 March 1912

Viscount Helmsley (seconding the opposition)

1.

I ~~maintain that the position and functions of Parli~~**am**~~ent would be altered… the fact of the two sexes sitting together in an assembly such as this would no doubt alter the whole tone and whole feeling of this Parliament.I do not think that any man will deny that he is conscious when he is debating in common with women of an extremely different feeling, a feeling of reserve, which is very different from the feeling which men have when they are discussing freely and debating freely with one another…~~

~~The way in which certain types of women, easily recognised, have acted in the last year or two, especially in the last few weeks, lends~~ **a** ~~great deal of colour to the argument that the mental equilibrium of the female sex is not as stable as the mental equilibrium of the~~ **male** ~~sex.The argument has very strong scientific backing… It seems to me that this House should remember that if the vote is given to women those who will take the greatest part~~ **in politics** ~~will not be the quiet, retiring, constitutional women… but those very militant women who have brought so much disgrace and discredit upon their sex. It would introduce~~ **a disastrous** ~~element into our public life… One feels that it is not cricket for women to use~~ **force**~~… It is little short of nauseating and disgusting to the whole sex…~~

~~Where are the women merchants and the women bankers? Where are the women directors of great undertakings? Nowhere to be seen at the head of the great businesses of the country. I can imagine very few undertakings in which women exercise an equal share of the control with the men… It appears to me that it is one of the fundamental truths on which all civilisations have been built up, that~~ **it is men who have made and controlled the State, and** ~~I cannot help thinking that any country which departs from that principle must be undertaking an experiment which in the end will~~ **prove to be exceedingly dangerous**~~…~~

~~I believe that the normal man and the normal women both have the instinct that man should be the governing one of the two, and I think that the undoubted dislike that women have for men who are effeminate and which men have for masculine women is nothing more or less than the expression of this instinct…~~

2.

~~I maintain that the whole position and functions of Parliament would be altered… the fact of the two sexes sitting together in an assembly such as this would no doubt alter the whole tone and whole feeling of this Parliament.I do not think that any man will deny that he is conscious when he is debating in common with women of an extremely different feeling, a feeling of reserve, which is very different from the feeling which men have when they are discussing freely and debating freely with one another…~~

~~The way in which certain types of women, easily recognised, have acted in the lastyear or two, especially in the last few weeks, lends a great deal of colour to the argument that the mental equilibrium of the female sex is not as stable as the mental equilibrium of the male sex.The argument has very strong scientific backing… It seems to me that this House should remember that if the vote is given to women those who will take the greatest part in politics will not be the quiet, retiring, constitutional women… but those very militant women who have brought so much disgrace and discredit upon their sex.It would introduce a disastrous element into our public life… One feels that it is not cricket for women to use force… It is little short of nauseating and disgusting to the whole sex…~~

~~Where are the women merchants and the women bankers? Where are the women directors of great undertakings? Nowhere to be seen at the head of the great businesses of the country. I can imagine very few undertakings in which women exercise an equal share of the control with the men… It appears to me that it is one of the fundamental truths on which all civilisations have been built up, that it is men who have made and controlled the State, and I cannot help thinking that any country which departs from that principle must be undertaking an experiment which in the end will prove to be exceedingly dangerous…~~

I believe that ~~the normal man and the normal~~ **women** ~~both have the instinct that man should be the governing one of the two, and I think that the undoubted dislike that women have for men who~~ **are** ~~effeminate and which men have for masculine women is nothing more or~~ **less than** ~~the expression of this instinct…~~

Thomas Jefferson. Excerpt from January 10, 1806: Address to the Chiefs of the Cherokee Nation

My children, ~~it is unnecessary for me to advise you against spending all your time and labor in warring with and destroying your fellow-men, and wasting your own members. You already see the folly and iniquity of it. Your young men, however, are not yet sufficiently sensible of it. Some of them cross the Mississippi to go and destroy people who have never done them an injury. My children, this is wrong and must not be; if we permit them to cross the Mississippi to war with the Indians on the other side of that river, we must let those Indians cross the river to take revenge on you. I say again, this must not be.~~ **The Mississippi now belongs to us.** ~~It must not be a river of blood. It is now the water-path along which all our people of Natchez, St. Louis, Indiana, Ohio, Tennessee, Kentucky and the western parts of Pennsylvania and Virginia are constantly passing with their property, to and from New Orleans. Young men going to war are not easily restrained. Finding our people on the river they will rob them, perhaps kill them. This would bring on a war between us and you. It is better to stop this in time by forbidding your young men to go across the river to make war. If they go to visit or to live with the Cherokees on the other side of the river we shall not object to that.~~ **That country is ours. We will** ~~permit them to live in it.~~

~~My children, this is what I wished to say to you. To go on in learning to cultivate the earth and to~~ **avoid** ~~war. If any of your neighbors injure you, our beloved men whom we place with you will endeavor to obtain~~ **justice** ~~for you and we will support them in it. If any of your bad people injure your neighbors,~~ **be ready** ~~to acknowledge it and~~ **to do** ~~them justice. It is more honorable to repair a~~ **wrong** ~~than~~ **to** ~~persist in it. Tell all~~ **your chiefs, your men, women and children**~~, that I take them by the hand and hold it fast. That I am their father, wish their happiness and well-being, and am always ready to promote their good.~~

~~My children, I thank you for your visit and pray to the Great Spirit who made us all and planted us all in this land to live together like brothers that He will conduct you safely to your homes, and grant you to find your families and your friends in good health.~~

In searching for texts I wanted to work with for this project, I focused on the words of 19th and early 20th century patriarchy—oppression of Native Americans, imperialist wars, women's suffrage. There was abundant material. It was depressing. Both speeches I eventually chose might seem absurd in the 21st century, certainly shocking, in their brazen paternalistic and misogynistic rhetoric. Of course, the attitudes, prejudices, and ideas remain, albeit somewhat better concealed (at least until the 2016 election) and perhaps even more pernicious because of that. I chose to use an erasure method that would leave the original, deeply disturbing texts legible, while revealing stark truth about the actions and beliefs represented in the speeches.

ZANN CARTER

18 U.S. Code § 2385 - Advocating overthrow of Government

I've always had a bit of a problem with authority, and now, in the current time, it's especially pronounced. This began somewhat as an exercise in my classroom—I bring students a variety of texts to practice erasure on, including pages from our student code of conduct, along with legal code pages. I began this to engage in the erasure process alongside my students and, perhaps because I was teaching, I was struck by the importance of teaching our children to be citizens to "form society" if we want a society that is worth having. And while I want to believe that peaceful revolution is possible, the first part of this piece speaks to the ever-growing temptation of the "by any means necessary" stance.

KI RUSSELL

"All the News
That's Fit to Print"

The New

VOL. CLXVI .... No. 57,656

NEW YORK,

NEWS ANALYSIS

Russia Story Refuses to Let The Page Turn

White House Rancor And Finger-Pointing

By PETER BAKER and MAGGIE HABERMAN

WASHINGTON — If President Trump emerged from his meeting with President Vladimir V. Putin of Russia last week hoping he had begun to "move forward" from the controversy over the Kremlin's election meddling, as advisers put it, his flight home the next day made clear just how overly optimistic that was.

As Air Force One jetted back from Europe on Saturday, a small cadre of Mr. Trump's advisers huddled in a cabin helping to craft a statement for the president's eldest son, Donald Trump Jr., to give to The New York Times explaining why he met last summer with a lawyer connected to the Russian government. Participants on the plane and back in the United States debated how transparent to be in the statement, according to people familiar with the discussions.

Ultimately, the people said, the president signed off on a statement from Donald Trump Jr. for The Times that was so incomplete that it required day after day of follow-up statements, each

ON JUN 3, 2016, AT 10:36 AM, ROB GOLDSTONE WROTE:
morning
called
met with hi
offered to provide
This is obviously
sensitiv
What do you think
speak
speak
love
Best,
Don

A Moscow Insider Trusted V

ork Times

Late Edition

Today, clouds and sunshine, afternoon showers or thunderstorms, humid, high 87. Tonight, cloudy, humid, low 74. Tomorrow, thunderstorms, high 91. Weather map, Page C8.

)AY, JULY 12, 2017 $2.50

ation would

is sensitive

ıoment

ıd if it's what you say

/inning Cases

EMAILS DISCLOSE TRUMP SON'S GLEE AT RUSSIAN OFFER

'I Love It,' He Said of Word of Documents Promised to Incriminate Clinton

This article is by **Jo Becker, Adam Goldman** *and* **Matt Apuzzo.**

The June 3, 2016, email sent to Donald Trump Jr. could hardly have been more explicit: One of his father's former Russian business partners had been contacted by a senior Russian government official and was offering to provide the Trump campaign with dirt on Hillary Clinton.

The documents "would incriminate Hillary and her dealings with Russia and would be very useful to your father," read the email, written by a trusted intermediary, who added, "This is obviously very high level and sensitive information but is part of Russia and its government's support for Mr. Trump."

If the future president's eldest son was surprised or disturbed by the provenance of the promised material — or the notion that it was part of a continuing effort by the Russian government to aid his father's campaign — he gave no indication.

He replied within minutes: "If it's what you say I love it especially later in the summer."

Four days later, after a flurry of

involved and what it was about. The story has unfolded as The Times has been able to confirm details of the meetings.

But the email exchanges, which were reviewed by The Times, offer a detailed unspooling of how the meeting with the Kremlin-connected Russian lawyer, Natalia Veselnitskaya, came about — and just how eager Donald Trump Jr. was to accept what he was explicitly told was the Russian government's help.

The Justice Department and the House and Senate Intelligence

SAM HODGSON FOR THE NEW YORK TIMES

Donald Trump Jr.

The New York T

656 © 2017 The New York Times Company NEW YORK, WEDNESDAY, JULY 12, 2017

ON JUN 3, 2016, AT 10:36 AM, ROB GOLDSTONE WROTE:

morning

called

met with his father

offered to provide

This is obviously sensitive

What do you think information would

speak

it is sensitive

at the moment

speak and if it's what you say

love

Best,

Don

A Moscow Insider Trusted With Winning Cases

I was working as a summer camp counselor on the day the infamous emails between Don Jr. and Rob Goldstone appeared on the front page of *The New York Times*. I had brought copies of newspapers with me to the camp that day intending to teach the children about erasure poetry. This was during our unit on political writing, and I instructed the children to choose articles that stood out to them as political. Maybe it's because I made this piece in the presence of children that it turns on the word "love," or maybe it's because the word seemed out of place. I ended up transforming the emails into something like a love poem. I enjoyed making them contradict themselves. I enjoyed, in the act of erasing their difference, exposing Rob Goldstone and Don Jr. as the same speaker.

SARAH GERARD

A Growing Crisis

My fellow Americans, tonight I'm a growing humanitarian and security crisis

Every day, we have no way to welcome millions of lawful immigrants who enrich our society and contribute to our nation,

I strain public resources and drive down jobs and wages. Among those hardest hit are Americans and Americans. Every week, our citizens are killed by our

officers

Over the years, thousands of Americans have been brutally killed and thousands more lives will be lost

This is a humanitarian crisis. A crisis of the heart, and a crisis of the soul. Last month, 20,000 migrant children were used as human pawns by our broken system.

This is the tragic reality of

My administration

It's a tremendous problem.

Our proposal

from homeland security includes cutting

lawful migration fueled by our very strong economy.

Furthermore, we have asked Congress to close

safe and humane

border security,

a concrete wall is absolutely

Vastly more than the $5.7 billion we have requested from Congress. The wall will also be

elected president.

Congress have refused to protect our families and

shut down My administration

This situation could be solved get this done. rise above partisan politics

why do wealthy politicians hate the people on the outside The only thing that is immoral is the politicians

America's heart broke savagely murdered

In California, In Georgia, In Maryland, in the United States

I have held weeping mothers and

stricken fathers.

gripping their souls. American blood shed

To every member of Congress: a crisis.

This is a choice between right and wrong, justice and injustice. This is about the American citizens. When I took the office, I swore to protect what will always help me.

Thank you and good night.

Source material: NYT Transcript of The President's Speech on Immigration, January 8, 2019 (https://www.nytimes.com/2019/01/08/us/politics/trump-speech-transcript.html)

"A Growing Crisis"* is based on Donald Trump's speech on immigration and border security on January 8, 2019. I've blocked out the extraneous words with a wall of bricks, leaving only enough room for the reality behind the fearmongering to peep through.

TARA CAMPBELL

* Previously published January 2019 in *Heavy Feather Review*.

From the Testimony of Dr. Karl Brandt at the Nuremburg Trials

October 1st, 1945

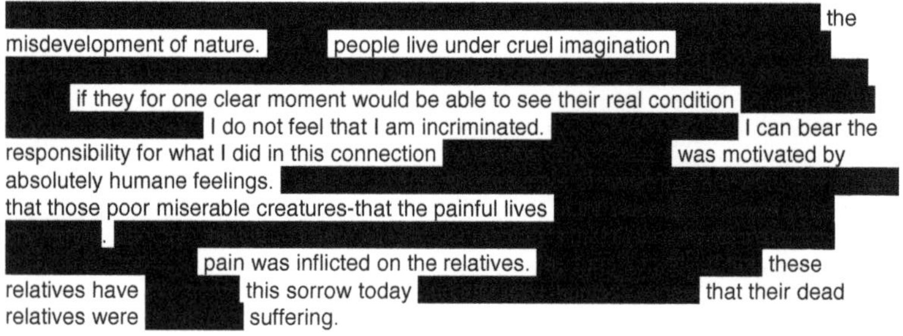
the
misdevelopment of nature. people live under cruel imagination
if they for one clear moment would be able to see their real condition
I do not feel that I am incriminated. I can bear the
responsibility for what I did in this connection was motivated by
absolutely humane feelings.
that those poor miserable creatures-that the painful lives
.
pain was inflicted on the relatives. these
relatives have this sorrow today that their dead
relatives were suffering.

July 19th, 1947

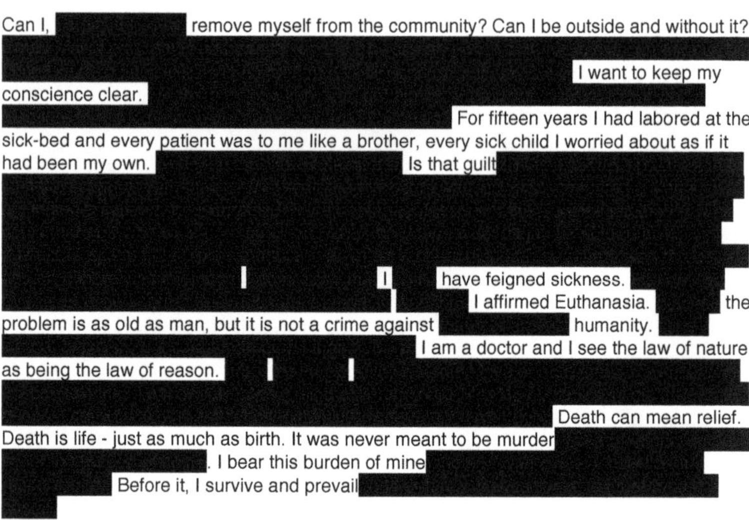
Can I, remove myself from the community? Can I be outside and without it?
I want to keep my
conscience clear.
For fifteen years I had labored at the
sick-bed and every patient was to me like a brother, every sick child I worried about as if it
had been my own. Is that guilt
I I have feigned sickness.
I affirmed Euthanasia. the
problem is as old as man, but it is not a crime against humanity.
I am a doctor and I see the law of nature
as being the law of reason. I I
Death can mean relief.
Death is life - just as much as birth. It was never meant to be murder
. I bear this burden of mine
Before it, I survive and prevail

August 21st, 1947, after receiving death sentence

the significance of death above execution
a medical experiment offering no chance of
survival. in

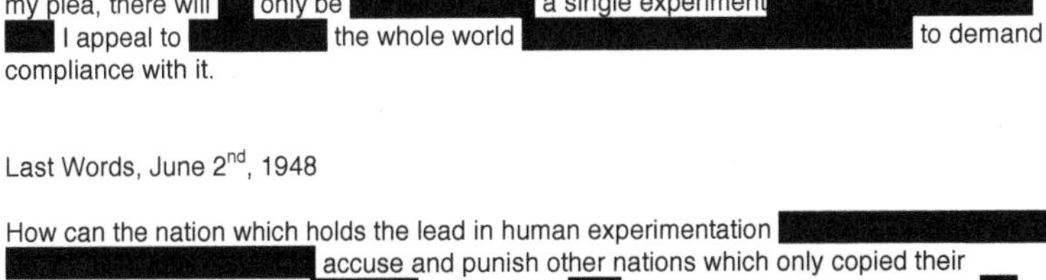
my plea, there will only be a single experiment I appeal to the whole world to demand compliance with it.

Last Words, June 2nd, 1948

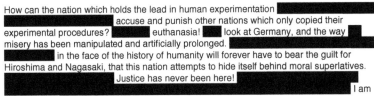

How can the nation which holds the lead in human experimentation accuse and punish other nations which only copied their experimental procedures? euthanasia! look at Germany, and the way misery has been manipulated and artificially prolonged. in the face of the history of humanity will forever have to bear the guilt for Hiroshima and Nagasaki, that this nation attempts to hide itself behind moral superlatives. Justice has never been here! I am such a victim.

I've always had a morbid fascination with the Holocaust. Growing up as a disabled, Jewish, gay, transgender girl, I learned about the Holocaust at around the same time I learned to read. As I grew into a deeper understanding of my identities, I began to imagine myself growing up in Nazi Germany. I had no direct relatives who were victims or survivors of the Holocaust, but friends' grandparents came to speak at school and synagogue about the horrors they endured. I knew if it happened again that there would be no chance, no hope for me. I saw the specter of the far-right rising again in the western world when I was young, and no one believed me. Here we are in a time where fascists are growing more and more emboldened to erase us from existence. I hate being right about things like this, and I pray every day to be proven wrong.

Dr. Karl Brandt was Hitler's personal doctor and one of two overseers of the Aktion T4 program, which involuntarily sterilized and euthanized some 300,000 disabled people between 1939 and 1945. He was not a villain from some horror movie or comic book—he was a real human being who saw his actions as justifiable in purifying the gene pool. In making my erasures from translations of his statements at the Nuremberg trials, I saw a fragile person with deep convictions who was utterly convinced of his own victimhood. In the blank spaces, in the silence underneath his words, he told the plain truth of the atrocities he committed. The deaths of hundreds of thousands of disabled adults and children were all to relieve the suffering of the perfect Aryan race. He was trying to put us all out of our misery by causing us unimaginable pain.

Here we are, seventy or so years after his death, with eugenics alive and fascism rising. There's nothing left for me to say; he said it all at Nuremberg.

TYLER VILE

REUTERS: But what would it look like?

PRUITT: It's in its formative stages. The idea is a good idea because it's an idea that advances science. It advances discussion. It advances transparency. It advances for the American people to consume and participate through this debate because there is not consensus on this issue. How do we know that? There has been no policy response. That's why we haven't seen Congress act because there has been such a question. It's not a question about whether warming is happening or whether we are contributing to it. That's not what we are debating. It's how much? To what degree? The precision of measurement. Does it pose a meaningful threat? Is it unsustainable? There is a host of questions that will be asked and answered during the process. It's exciting.

When I found out about this erasure project, I knew I wanted to write about the men in charge of the natural resource agencies in the Trump administration. I have worked in different federal agencies focused on natural resource management and was horrified (though not surprised) when oil barons were hired on as department heads. I watched decades of hard work done by people on the ground wiped away. It was infuriating, to say the least. But it wasn't just personal exasperation that drove me to create these erasures. I'm deeply concerned about Scott Pruitt's enactment of environmental violence. Exploitation of the land inherently results in harm to marginalized communities, whether through direct means (forced removal, physical violence, suppression of information) or through indirect effects (pollution-borne disorders, competition for resources, etc.).

For the erasure, I decided to select a passage from an interview Pruitt did concerning his beliefs on human-caused climate change. He has famously denied the reality of climate change and promoted deregulation of oil and gas industries, the top generators of greenhouse gases. Because of his actions, we are even closer to irreversible climatic catastrophe, risking the lives of billions of people, largely people who have already suffered at the hands of patriarchal and colonial systems of oppression.

The erasure here was done on a printed copy of Pruitt's interview. My original intention was to only use potting soil to do the erasure. However, I found that it wasn't the best at covering up the original words, so I paired the dirt with brown marker to create a "dirty" effect in the erasure.

ASHELY ADAMS

Erasure from "The Declaration of Independence"

The political powers are men.
Consent is disposed
by a long train of abuses,
a repeated tyranny. Over these states,
he has refused the most necessary laws,
suspended their operation.
Neglected the right of legislative bodies,
of the people. He, elected, the danger
of these states. Obstructing justice
for power and payment,
he has kept consent foreign.
He has plundered, ravaged, burned
out people. This desolation
scarcely paralleled. The head of our country
the executioner. Merciless. Unfit.
People have been warned, appealed to.
They have been deaf to the voice of justice.
We the people, united, are dissolved.

[author's statement is the erasure]

RACHEL SUCHER

JOURNALISM & MEDIA

"build new men and burn the old ones down"

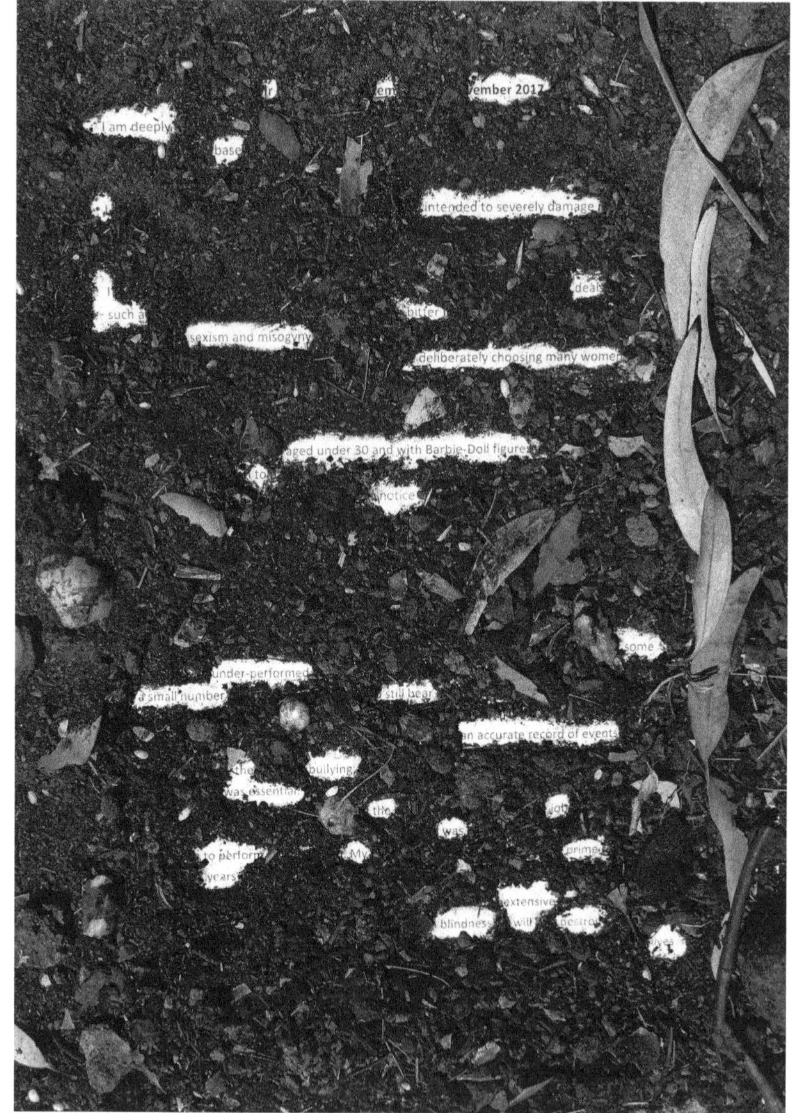

ember 2017
I am deeply
base
intended to severely damage
deal
such a
bitter
sexism and misogyny
deliberately choosing many women
aged under 30 and with Barbie-Doll figures
to
notice
some
under-performed
a small number
still bear
an accurate record of events
the
bullying
was essential
the
job
was
to perform
My
prime
years
extensive
blindness
will
destro
ives

my
intentionally destructive
behaviour
has been
working out
very safe and
very happy to
me
this
"Weinstein" moment
is unfair and unworthy
would never tolerate
court
There are others
Don Burke
26 November 2017

This erasure, "remember 2017," is of a public statement made in November 2017 by an Australian ex-TV host and producer, Don Burke, after multiple women came forward accusing him of harassment and assault in the late 1980s and early 1990s.

His statement claims none of it ever happened and complains about the harm to his current charity activities and lucrative public appearance work. The full text of his statement, and details of the allegations, are detailed in this news story: http://www.abc.net.au/news/2017-11-27/don-burke-accused-of-sexual-harassment-indecent-assault/9188070.

While largely unknown in the United States, Don Burke is a household name in Australia. It is interesting to note how the Weinstein / #MeToo moment has played out in other places around the world. The Weinstein revelations were definitely a factor in the news story appearing when it did, and Burke references Weinstein's case twice in his own statement.

The TV program Don Burke hosted and produced (*Burke's Backyard*) ran for 18 years in prime time on a major network and was a phenomenal success. It was also, incidentally, a gardening show. Accordingly, poet Melinda Smith decided to do the erasure with soil. She liked the additional echoes of contamination—and also burial and exhumation—because the original complaints against Burke were 'buried' by his network for so long.

To achieve the finished piece, Melinda first worked with Burke's statement in Word, blocking out chunks from the text to leave behind a much more frank admission than the original. She printed it out A3 size (as two A4 pages side-by-side), taped it to an old coffee table, and covered it completely in soil and compost. Frequent collaborator visual artist Caren Florance then helped 'excavate' in the right places (navigating the 'dig' by using a clean copy of the redacted statement) to reveal the desired words. Caren also took the photographs. Below, for reference, is the text of the erasure (as the photographic version can be a little difficult to read in places).

REMEMBER 2017

I am deeply base.
I intended to severely damage.

I deal such a bitter
sexism and misogyny.
deliberately choosing many women
aged under 30 and with Barbie-Doll figures
to notice

some under-performed

a small number still bear
an accurate record of events.

the bullying was essential.
the job was to perform My prime years.

extensive blindness will destroy lives.

my intentionally destructive behaviour
has been working out very safe
and very happy to me so far.

this "Weinstein" moment
is unfair and unworthy.

I would never tolerate court.

There are others.

Don Burke
26 November 2017

CAREN FLORANCE AND MELINDA SMITH

sorry for any humiliation
I have caused my
customers

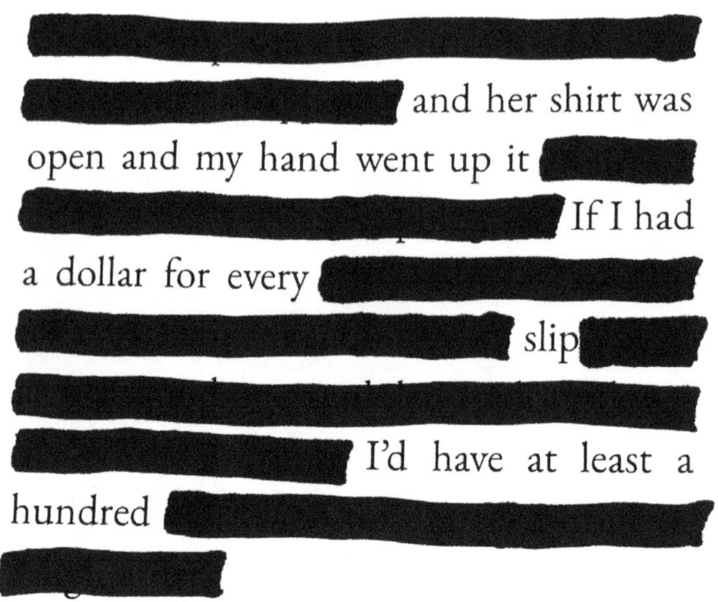

and her shirt was
open and my hand went up it
If I had
a dollar for every
slip
I'd have at least a
hundred

GARRISON KEILLOR

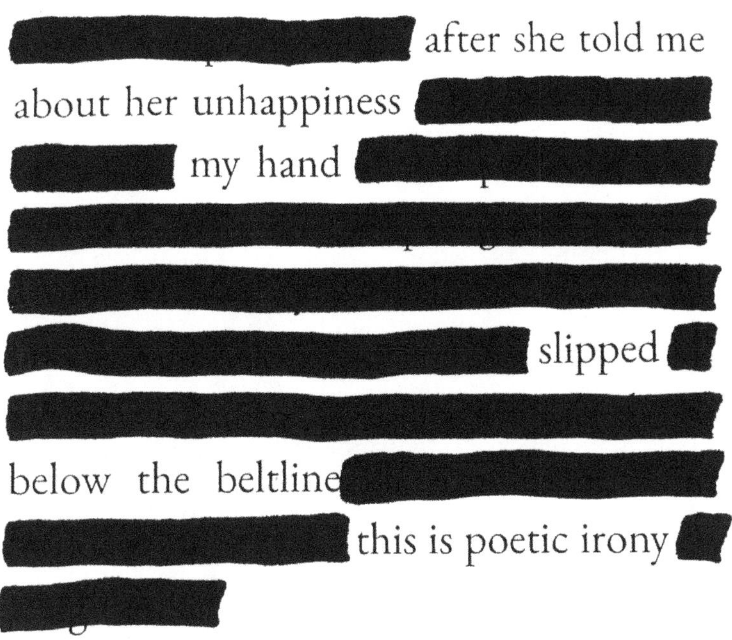

after she told me
about her unhappiness
my hand
slipped
below the beltline
this is poetic irony

GARRISON KEILLOR

After I worked on these erasures, I went home to Michigan for Christmas and discussed them with my family.

Batali's "apology" reeked of overt concern for his brand, and I felt compelled to highlight its most capitalist moment: when the arrogant chef apologizes to his *customers*. One relative, who I deeply respect, seemed to feel that Batali had gotten a raw deal. I asked him over apple pie one night, "Have you ever honked the breasts of a female coworker?"

"I've never done anything like that to any woman, ever in my life," he said.

"Well?" I asked. "Doesn't that make you think?"

"Let me tell you what," he continued, "Batali said he was a much younger man when this happened. You know how it is," he chortled. In that brief laugh, I heard his dismissal as clearly as if he'd shouted it.

When I told this relative that Keillor had always creeped me out, he turned to me sharply and asked, "Now why would you say a thing like that?" He listened to Keillor on long drives in the Arizona desert while test driving cars for GM in the 1970s. As a woman, my gut feelings are less useful than nostalgia, I suppose.

Keillor seemed strangely unable to avoid talking in corporeal terms about his victim's body and her "unhappiness." His felt like an admission, and my erasures purposely conflate this confession with his victim blaming (and hints, as his language already does, that he's done this before).

CAITLIN COWAN

One Nice Thing

One nice thing about being a social pariah is that no political candidates will ever ask me for money again and **nobody will invite me to speak at** commencement ever. I spoke to a **women**'s book club in Osseo a couple weeks ago. I will never be asked to do such a thing **again**. This means I may be able to sit down and read Moby Dick.

Source: Garrison Keillor's Facebook post (friends) - 12.1.17

I met Garrison Keillor and took a selfie with him at my university in 2016. When he was fired in 2017, I read several of his statements about the allegations against him. This one was a friends-only Facebook post. I grayed out the entire text and then highlighted the words that seemed to capture an honest subtext, as if Keillor were giving a dramatic monologue and revealing his true nature despite himself.

KATIE MANNING

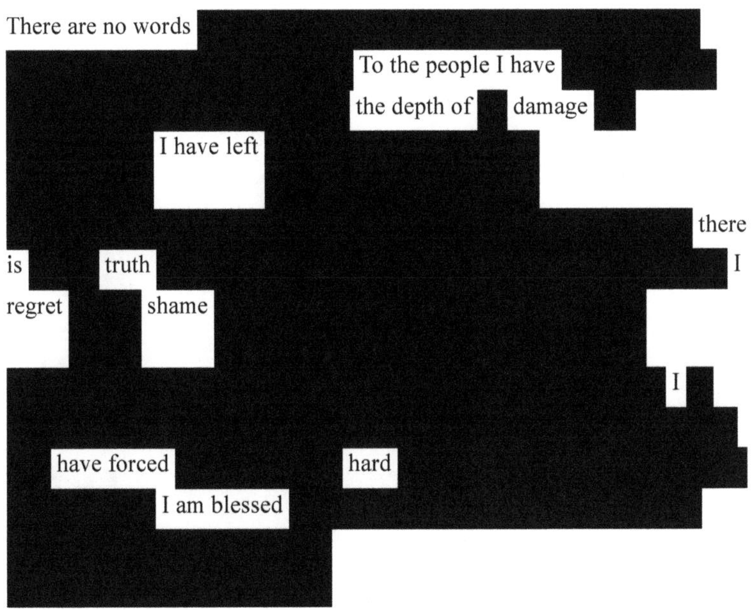
There are no words
To the people I have
the depth of damage
I have left
there
is truth I
regret shame
I
have forced hard
I am blessed

With Matt Lauer's apology, I sought to black out parts that I felt were filler speech and lines he "knew" he had to say and wanted to illustrate the emptiness of his words and the true depths of his actions. Powerful people in position, especially men like Lauer, hardly have to face real consequences that ruin their lives, especially in comparison to the destruction and horror he caused others. To me, he felt more upset about being publicly caught than he did for truly hurting people. To me, there is a huge difference between a heartfelt, authentic apology that takes accountability, as opposed to cobbling some words together to appear apologetic.

JOANNA C. VALENTE

let's be clear what is happening here.

I

don't care about victims, only

about me

I am

offensive, and

oppressive

I will never stop

I was a street medic for the protesters on the fiery UC Berkeley campus the day Milo Yiannopoulos came to town. I've known of Milo for years, mainly because I lived in London where he got his trollish start, and also because I have many female friends who worked in the gaming community. Milo helped make their lives a living hell through online harassment, then came to the United States to help ensure the Alt Right could have their little reign of terror. I chose him for this piece because I've had to help manage the wreckage he and his cronies have left behind, and I'm done cleaning up after his tantrums.

KITTY STRYKER

Bullying

Antonio Caballero, 12/16/2017, *Semana*

God, all these powerful men, like Donald Trump, film producers,
congressmen,
you really have an average erection

You have to be very sick very stupid to be exalted
in the United States
It is true that

Sixteen women, and they should be more, are accusing Donald Trump of sexual abuse
he touched their ass or tit: , yes, vulgar
sexual abuse, which is serious.
knock down the president of the United States for that
which is certainly true The president of the United States deserves to be dismissed for
sexual
abuse rudeness and bullying.
rude bully voters chose him to
see him physically threaten Hillary Clinton
in the election their
women, their children.

in talking about violations
an actress A secretary
A beauty queen
protest the
president,
the patriarchal and chauvinistic
president

let's not exaggerate. sexual assault is macho harassment. Trying to kiss without being invited is impalement. a libidinous look, criminal

That this is the usual, the normal thing, is precisely what reveals the existence of a patriarchal and macho culture in contemporary society.

sexual abuse banalizes and excuses sexual innuendo unacceptable sexual intention sexual criminal s , and yes, Hollywood and Washington

(Note: those who ask for excuses. It is a crime.

Harassment

Antonio Caballero, 12/23/2017, *Semana*

It is very clear that I am defending the aggressors; I am criticizing the victims

My column last week on sexual harassment provoked many protests and my misogyny, my inveterate machismo, the fact that I am a white and powerful man

did defend sexual abusers like Harvey Weinstein and Donald Trump it condemned the serious It is not just that, it is also bad education.

in the discussion these days about Hollywood and the president We are talking about

a paradigm of sexual abuse Or, more pertinently

that men lack in these matters because they lack empathy.

Undoubtedly there is some

point of view, which is that other men

do not consider women inferior

it is very clear that defending the aggressors

in these specific cases

is taking place in the unjust society in which we live. A macho and patriarchal society

feminist and matriarchal society

mean s progress with respect

At the end of 2017, as the #MeToo movement spread globally, Colombian columnist Antonio Caballero denounced female journalists who were speaking out about sexual assault. In two of his columns, he said women should quit whining and draw attention to more important things.

As I read his words in the online version of *Semana*, the Colombian weekly magazine he writes for, I reflected on what it is to be a Hispanic woman: silent, enduring. In fact, a month after Caballero's columns were published, journalist Claudia Morales published an account of her rape, saying she had to protect her father's job and her future, so she had said nothing at the time.

Fucking machismo, I thought. But I understood. As a Colombian-American, I spent much of my youth in Bogotá, where men would say and mimic all kinds of sexual things as I passed on the street. "Don't say anything to them," was always my Colombian mother's response. "Don't even look at them."

After Caballero's second column drew criticism, he appeared on a Colombian radio program, defending himself. I listened to his pathetic excuses, appalled. "I tried to say that feminism and machismo can exist together, peacefully," he said. "But you misunderstood."

No. We did not misunderstand.

In the same way a twelve-year-old girl knows what it means when a man pumps his hips at her, readers understood Caballero's words.

With these erasures, I wanted to confront this man and make him speak the truth he cannot understand.

MARCELLA PROKOP

I don’t think

If you’re asking transgender or
plus-size ,
Why ?

I
don’t think .

"I don't think" is an erasure of Edward Razek's (senior creative at Victoria's Secret) statement after he was called out for not allowing transgender or plus-size models to be a part of the VS show. The more the patriarchy tries to explain itself—behaviors, reactions, etc.—the further it gets from the truth. This erasure poem is an attempt to uncover the truth that is being muddled by Razek's statement. The truth is never too far, even when someone tries to conceal it.

ELIZABETH SCHMUHL

Between Men

the promise

of power,
on the backs of our children.

the reasons
for this are clear.

Our quest to stand and impose on
the human experience
sex-based power

We have become obsessed with
the other.

we have ambitions
mistrust, animosity and ignorance

Building Men in the 21st Century

For years the fair and equitable men stand without the burden of sex.

By meaningful gender we remove the expectations of children. Such is our fairness.

Fifty years only realized the opposite of reason

Our quest to impose powerlessness has devolved into women. We have become indifferent, even hostile

The result of fate is

Rather egalitarian; the sex we have twisted into a chasm. Rather than building better men, we have contented ourselves with burning

Conference on Men's

Women

in Houston, Texas we will correct

honest dialogue;

elbow out

female power. succinctly, we are talking about

women, a cost

vital for sex

row ahead we have both oars

Men
in the 1st Century

---

the promise

of sex.

expectation of
future opportunity.

years later those reasons
are clear.

Our limitations impose
goals
evolve into a rigid

struggle
hostile

unite the
equals, we have ambitions
build new
men and burn
the old ones down.

In 2015, Men's Rights Activist Paul Elam announced the second International Conference on Men's Issues on his website *A Voice for Men* in a post titled "ICMI 15: Building Bridges Between Men and Women in the 21st Century." The first ICMI had been held the year prior in Detroit and received all sorts of coverage in the mainstream media—in large part, coverage that clearly aimed to be "fair and balanced" and to humanize the movement's participants even if condemning their hateful, dangerous rhetoric. The announcement for the 2015 conference suggests that feminism erases the concerns of men by focusing solely on gains for women: "We cannot limp forward as a society on concerns for only one sex, just as we cannot advance as two equal sexes by continuing to address the problems of only one of them." Ironically, this erases (or, at best, ignores) the feminist voices that have over and over identified the ways patriarchy harms men, too, and prescribed feminism as a balm for all our wounds.

I erased the announcement because I'm tired of media coverage that humanizes dehumanizers. I erased it because my erasures strip down the rhetoric to its obvious misogyny. I erased it because the movement incites hatred and violence and should be less visible. And I erased it to draw attention to what it erases.

The 2015 International Conference on Men's Issues was canceled by *A Voice for Men* due to "staff burnout." It has taken place yearly since then. There has been less media coverage.

KRISTA COX

CHAD GRIFFIN FORMALLY APOLOGIZES

many millions of dollars put into

a gesture

a deeper

sinking We all know why

I I

I formally apologize.

I am sorry

I am sorry for you

people

I I

I I

I

will change

enough

CHAD GRIFFIN NOTICES A TRANS

I'm here
because
A few months ago
I
noticed
a trans
I had no idea
before that night
finding comfort
in
progress
Despite
discrimination

CHAD GRIFFIN WANTS TO BE HELD ACCOUNTABLE

These three pieces are erasures of HRC (Human Rights Campaign) president Chad Griffin's public apology to trans people for the organization's shitty treatment/erasure of us in the past, which was given as a speech at Southern Comfort.

When I read the call for submissions to *Erase the Patriarchy*, my first thought was to erase the statement of a more major-league piece of shit: a Louis C.K. or a Kevin Spacey, for example. But there are so many that I couldn't decide, so I figured I'd wait and see what came to me. I scrolled through Facebook and saw an ad demanding that I donate money to the Human Rights Campaign. That's when I remembered Griffin's apology, which I'd encountered after someone shared *The Advocate*'s published transcript of it in 2014. This was when I'd just moved from the South to Boston, and before I was living as an out trans person, before I had the language with which to process and describe my identity/experiences. I watched part of the accompanying video of Griffin speaking, and it was like watching a televangelist. Friendly. Enthusiastic. Empty. The apology made me angry.

I sent it to a friend, expecting her to talk shit about it with me, but she didn't get it. *Idk it seems nice to me*, she said, *he's trying*. This was frustrating. The fact that it *seems nice* and that *he's trying* is precisely what angered me. *Trying* didn't fix my intense dysphoria or reassure me when I felt like suicide was the only option I had. *Trying* didn't change public opinion. *Trying* didn't bring people back to life or give people money / shelter / food / healthcare / safety / dignity / confidence / validation / love / etc. I knew I couldn't expect a speech to do or promise those things. Yet, in a way, I somehow did expect it to. And I felt even more upset that someone I trust and care about was unable to see what I saw or to imagine what I did or to just listen. I couldn't explain my thoughts or my pain in a meaningful way. I felt helpless and stupid.

I see that fucking yellow equals sign all the time: in my email, on social media, stuck on laptops and bathroom stall walls and poles on the T. But I don't feel safe or comforted by it. I see that symbol and I think of all the other variations of Chad Griffin out there, the Chad Griffins who think that the fact they have "seen" or talked to (*at*, most likely) trans people means that they're extremely woke, that they're no longer "part of the problem," that they've earned the right to flaunt to everyone how tolerant and progressive they are. These same Chad Griffins who misgender me and then get so emotional when I correct them that it turns into me apologizing to them for wanting basic respect.

Who tell me that "it makes sense" that my health insurance required me to be on testosterone for a year (even though it's not medically necessary) before approving top surgery "so people don't rush into it." Who stare at me on the train and at work and at the gym and at parties and at the library and in the grocery store. Who hear a drunk man call me a faggot and say nothing. It is beyond annoying to me when these Chad Griffins get so much support and praise for saying that they finally learned that trans people exist/matter, when they have done the bare minimum, which they were often forced to do. When actual trans people who express themselves often get the opposite of support or nothing or don't even get the opportunity to speak to begin with.

I'm not saying that the Human Rights Campaign doesn't do important work or that cis people aren't allowed to evolve their knowledge and understanding of gender. I'm saying that Chad Griffin is not a hero for saying he's now a decent human. I'm saying that you are not a hero for giving $5 one time to the HRC and slapping the yellow equals sign on your Nalgene. I am saying that his apology is not for trans people. It is for cis people who want to feel good about themselves. Who want to feel like they've earned that shiny sticker without doing anything difficult.

What I left on the page is what I felt I was reading when I first read the apology, best summed up using Griffin's own words: "Please / fight / I won't / protect / you."

SALLY BURNETTE

RELIGION

"the foulest abominations"

The Bull of Innocent VIII

The Bull of Innocent VIII

afflict and torment men

whenc

they do not shrink from

perpetrating the foulest abominations

These erasures came out of what I imagine as a knot of roots within me, someplace dark and moist where the living feeds from. I've been working on a project that began as an exploration of herbal birth control, and has since expanded into an investigation of witchcraft, colonialization, and the intersections of personal and bioregional health. The Bull of Innocent is where a 'witch' was first defined in Western Europe—this definition is more an act of explaining what a witch did.

I found myself drawn to the bull for many reasons. I wanted to plant a garden out of it. I'm a witch, and I do a lot of work with herbs. I feel most powerful outside, in all kinds of weather and elements. Patriarchy doesn't support this power. It doesn't support what it can't control. Patriarchy holds a deep fear of Keats' negative capability. It fears a witch and works to suppress, oppress, or kill that power. I liken this power to what Audre Lorde calls 'The Erotic as Power,' or what Buffy Sainte-Marie sings of in 'God Is Alive Magic Is Afoot.'

The idea that this bull could be rewritten and subverted to become the very thing the writer worked to rid the world of is a form of witchcraft. Reading it was witchy. Destroying it was witchy. Creating from it is witchy. I let myself create these erasures from that unknown space. I think what I wanted was to make a garden, something beautiful where I could imagine people thriving. Of course, witchcraft has been oversimplified in our culture. While we're reclaiming the witch archetypes, what we do have available still tends to be simplified.

It seems both pieces work for me as a spell would. One serves to bring about desired intentions, the other serves as a hex. What I'm doing is not enough; there is a polarity in them, and reality to much too complex for polarities. However, it's a start, and that's how I've settled into living. Starting the work, and going from there. Dreaming and living my dreams to the best of my capabilities, then letting the dream tell me what it needs. I find dreams know more of what we need than we do.

GENEVIEVE PFEIFFER

obedience

to

Faith.

is

to

deny

hunger

men

are

diseases

And

God

is

man

truth

is

heresy,

fabricated

by

devils.

daughters created

for

men

discover

devils

witch

make a

grave

of

temptation.

face

the devil

The text chosen for this erasure project is Malleus Maleficarum (*Hammer of Witches*), written in 1487 by Heinrich Kramer and Jacob Sprenger.

I chose this text because I could, and I erased it because I could.

CALLIE GILL

SCIENCE & EDUCATION

"the guilt that men deny"

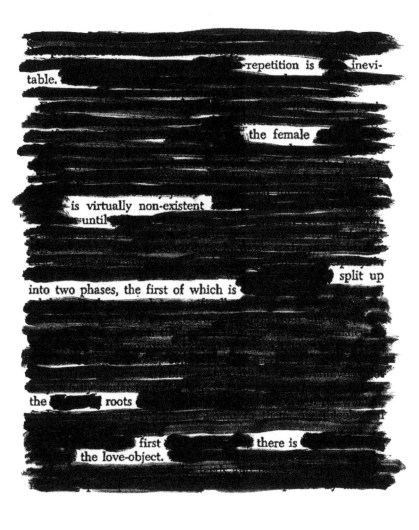

repetition is inevi-
table.

the female

is virtually non-existent
until

split up
into two phases, the first of which is

the roots

first there is
the love-object.

This redaction is from Sigmund Freud's essay *Female Sexuality* (1931), which focuses largely on the concept of penis envy and casts the female body (and, by extension, the psyche) as objectively inferior ("She acknowledges the fact of her castration, the consequent superiority of the male and her own inferiority, but she also rebels against these unpleasant facts"). As a woman who has experienced lifelong anxiety and depression, the field of psychology has always fascinated me, as has the knowledge that this field is, from its origins, deeply entrenched in misogyny. There's something almost unsettlingly whimsical about the misogyny of Freud, his insistence on viewing human anatomy as a functional metaphor of absence and presence, his medicalization and subsequent validation of gendered power structures, the whole hideous boys' club of leather armchairs, academia, and the privilege inherent in being able to declare that sometimes pipes are just pipes if they're yours and you don't want them to mean something you find uncomfortable. In short, I'm sort of creeped out by the fact that the lens my own psychological issues are viewed through was at least partially constructed via dubiously-academic essays as insane as Freud's *Female Sexuality*, so it felt pretty good to render it down to its core reductive thesis via erasure.

CHELSEA MARGARET BODNAR

MARITAL FREQUENCY

Do women desire ?
can
urge
b e full of
otherhood

women
rain

as
desire

If the woman
has

a
deep
op
al

long
ing

how much
til the
a c h e s

end this
vigorous

Source: *A Doctor's Marital Guide for Patients: Rhythm Edition* by Bernard R. Greenblat, M.D. (The Budlong Press, 1957).

WE

master the art of sex

break the rhythm of

er uption

hold

the motion of readiness

the n

study the se a

Sex can

sing

the drudgery that

marriage cannot

smooth

The key is to

s e a r

t he rust

pressed in t o

"will you want to use me tonight?"

Source: *A Doctor's Marital Guide for Patients: Rhythm Edition* by Bernard R. Greenblat, M.D. (The Budlong Press, 1957).

I have been working on this manuscript for almost eight years now, doing most of the blackouts by hand. I decided to try erasing the text on the computer for a change of pace. It allowed me to zoom in, erasing not just words but parts of words, sometimes leaving just one letter to spell new words. Each time I approach a new page, I skim it and see what words jump out at me, then I circle them and start to create a narrative. The poem usually reveals itself during that process. Much of what I've learned from using this text is that the doctor actually used a lot of brilliant language, so it was fun to try to condense each page to just a few words.

LAURA DESIANO

piously [illegible] questionable revelations they encountered [illegible] something like [illegible] just what I [illegible] knew [illegible] I knew [illegible] all along [illegible] the ig[illegible] of the Dark Ages [illegible] muddy the [illegible] waters. No one ever took the [illegible] as [illegible] were feeling [illegible] not feeling [illegible] ual [illegible] they [illegible] tion [illegible] would [illegible] cow [illegible] woman.

Did these experts do any harm?

Only to women. Most of the early "facts" about female sexual behavior consisted entirely of male wishful thinking. Little things about women not really being capable of enjoying sex and [illegible] being sexually superior to women began to appear [illegible] textbooks with [illegible] regularity. As the same [illegible] tions and misunderstandings were repeated over and over again, they began to take on the veneer of [illegible]. As one expert repeated [illegible] scientific [illegible] to another [illegible] rs took on the aura of authority. [illegible] found their way into magazines and [illegible] became part of [illegible] sexual folk-lore. [illegible] relentless repetition they finally achieved [illegible] acceptance as facts.

H[illegible] affect [illegible]

Because there is such [illegible] honest authoritative information about [illegible] sex [illegible] women are the most avid seekers of knowledge [illegible] their own [illegible] lives. They devour every scrap of information about their sexual selves. Although what they read was mostly bad news, it was (or so they thought) better than no news at all. As they were bombarded again and again with the same dubious information about female sexuality, they began to believe it. Even worse, they gradually developed the "cops and robbers syndrome."

[illegible] robbers syndrome"?

Policemen and criminals, in their spare time, watch television. They see how their video counterparts operate and, like the rest of us, tend to [illegible] (consciously or unconsciously) the behavior depicted on the screen. Subsequently, when a TV [illegible] to film a show about police and crooks, in a bid for [illegible] he bases his research [illegible] actual responses of real individuals. [illegible] fortunately for him, [illegible] subjects already have adopted [illegible] characteristics of the actors who portray them on television. The [illegible] show only succeeds in perpetuating the stereotype it was attempting [illegible]

How [illegible] that person [illegible]

As women are deluged [illegible] reliable accounts of how they behave (or should [illegible] sexually, they gradually adapt their sexual responses [illegible] to correspond with the accounts they have read. It becomes a case of reality imitating fantasy—with the woman coming out on the losing end. Not only do women act as if all the myths written about them were true, they pass the bad news on to their daughters who make it part of their own lives and in turn inflict it on their daughters. Carried to its ultimate absurd conclusion, the result is a generation of women who have accepted as facts [illegible] collection of sexual rumors, misconceptions, misunderstandings, and just plain old masculine wishful thinking.

"Masculine wishful thinking [illegible]

Yes. Each man has his own private sets of fears and anxieties about sex. Part of it is the result of the tremendous burden of guilt that our society imposes on every child—boy and girl—long before they have their first sexual stirring. The other factor that works against men is their relentless attempt to deny their unquestionable *functional sexual inferiority.*

The erasure “Robbers Syndrome” is from *Any Woman Can!* by David Reuben, MD—advertised as an address to women who are looking for love and sexual fulfillment. However, like most texts written by men for women, Dr. Rueben fails to consider the societal inequities, attitudes, and gendered violence against his desired audience that would at the very least examine how women are, in his words, “sexually marooned.” Furthermore, Dr. Rueben ignores any non-heteronormative sexual relationships, upholding the asymmetrical power dynamic between men and women, and emphasizing women’s responsibility to “alleviate the sexual insecurities of the male.”

As a queer writer, I wanted to destabilize the expectation of sex as power struggle through erasing the informal question-and-answer structure that serves to situate Dr. Rueben as an authority over women’s sexuality, blotting out the question of “what is cops and robbers syndrome” until only “robbers syndrome” is visible. I chose whiteout over a medium that completely obscures the underlying text because I wanted the reader to discern portions of the context to mirror how women have had to exist inside male-defined narratives—women as robber, as robbed. The dissolution of connective lines from the left to right side of the page demonstrates how women navigate male-constructed landscapes of femininity and reflect how men are the ones sexually isolated, marooned, through this silencing.

MEG E. GRIFFITTS

Chris Sacca: No Imbalance of Power

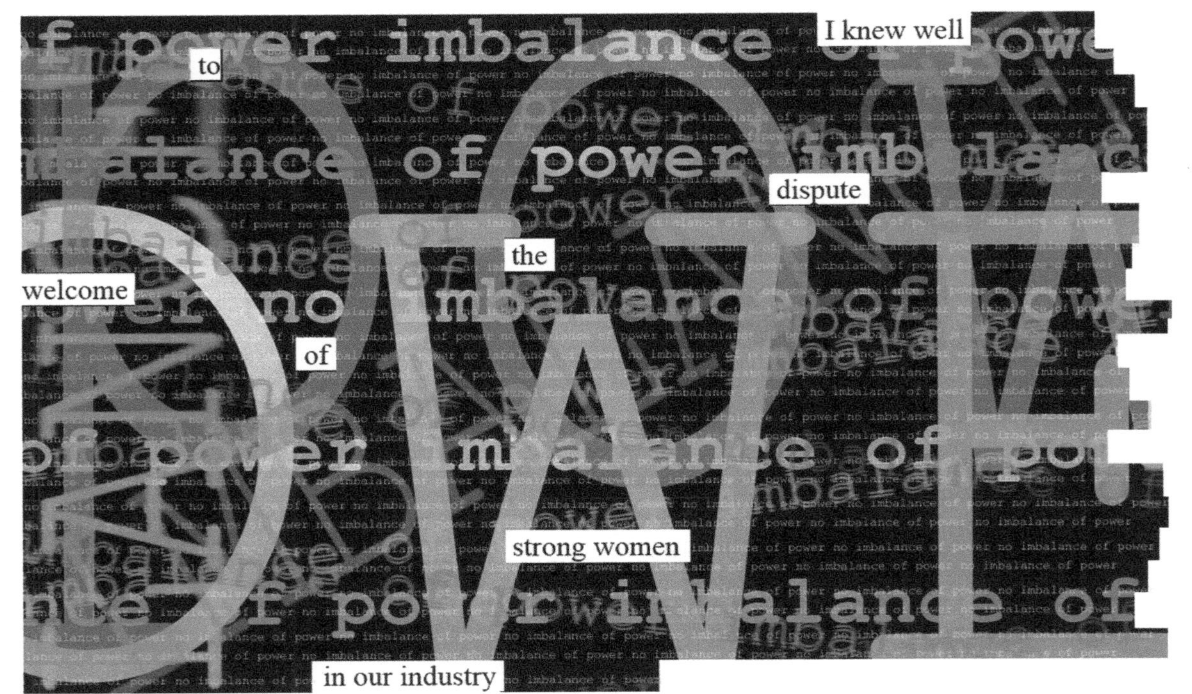

Eric Schmidt: Unconscious Bias

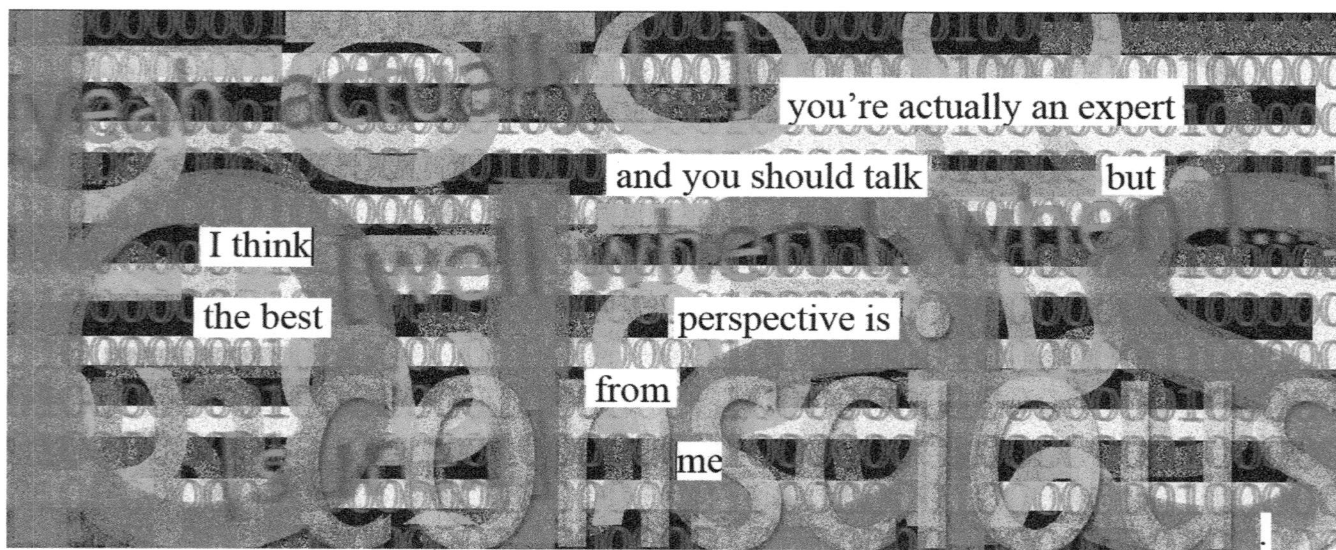

you're actually an expert
and you should talk
but
I think
the best
perspective is
from
me

In the technology world, abusive power dynamics situate women both as the targets of overt misogyny and collateral damage of bias. These erasure pieces highlight underlying messages of toxic technology culture in both the remaining poem text and negative space.

"NO IMBALANCE OF POWER"

After venture capitalist Chris Sacca apologized for "inhospitable" treatment of women entrepreneurs on *Medium*, in a post titled, "I Have More Work To [sic] Do," he reframed a woman's accusation of him, revising his apology by insisting "[t]here was no imbalance of power between us." My erasure reveals the entrenched culture of making women unwelcome in this field by upholding the premise that women owe their male colleagues.

"UNCONSCIOUS BIAS"

In 2015, former Google executive Eric Schmidt participated in a SXSW panel discussion, "How Innovation Happens" with Megan Smith, then Chief Technology Officer for the Obama administration. During the conversation, Schmidt repeatedly interrupted and talked over Smith, despite her attempts to interject with her own perspective. Schmidt admitted the Chief Technology Officer to be the actual expert on topics while he continued to dominate the discussion. At the end of the talk, audience member and Global Diversity and Talent Programs manager at Google, Judith Williams, called out Schmidt for his "unconscious bias" in interrupting Smith. This piece blurs Smith's interjections with the streams of 1s and 0s below the poem extracted from Schmidt's monologue, asking the question—does the bias remain *un*conscious? Or does "manterrupting" represent more calculated silencing?

ELISABETH MEHL GREENE

The effort by the United Auto Workers to unionize graduate and undergraduate students who serve as teaching and research assistants elicits strong views in and outside our community for understandable reasons. At stake, from the perspective of those seeking to establish a union, are promises of higher compensation and improved benefits. Others among us are deeply concerned about what it means to have an outside party involved in what are ultimately academic and intellectual judgments by faculty members.

We are announcing today our decision not to engage in bargaining with union representatives and to seek review of the status of student assistants by a federal appellate court. We recognize the potential, indeed the likelihood, for disappointment and dispute in our community. Needless to say, we have not come to this decision lightly. Because of the principles at stake—principles essential to the University's mission of training scholars—we have declined to bargain until the legal process has been allowed to run its course. We remain convinced that the relationship of graduate students to the faculty that instruct them must not be reduced to ordinary terms of employment. It is a conviction that, in the end, made this admittedly difficult decision straightforward for us. While the National Labor Relations Board's position on student assistants has shifted repeatedly with changes in political administrations, the University's view has remained constant, as has our well-established record of collective bargaining with the several unions that appropriately represent thousands of Columbia employees.

Our concern for these principles and for safeguarding the University's mission exists alongside our acknowledgment of the concerns students have expressed during the period of union organizing. This is why we have been working productively with the Graduate Student Advisory Council, the Engineering Graduate Student Council, and other student government bodies to address stipend and quality of life issues, and why we will continue to do so. Indeed, within a short time, the University will be announcing a series of new enhancements for graduate students.

In past communications to you about unionization, I have said that we are determined to improve the experience of research and teaching assistants at Columbia because we want to continue to attract the very best graduate students in the world. Our current research and teaching assistants belong to that group of world-class students and future scholars. We have made a lasting commitment to your future, want you to thrive intellectually and personally while you are here, and, therefore, are deeply invested in addressing your concerns. I look forward to continuing to work with you—and for you—in pursuit of these goals.

Here, I have overwritten a statement by Columbia University provost John Coatsworth, in which he announces that the university plans to break the law by refusing to bargain with its graduate workers union after the union was certified by the National Labor Relations Board. In the space surrounding the erasure, I've written over his text with my own statement addressing the university as a member of its graduate workforce, as well as with quotations from a document written by a group of women explaining the connection between the labor injustices at Columbia and the school's chronic problems with sexual harassment and assault. In honor of my organizer colleagues who have always strived to cut through the bureaucratic doublespeak, I have left spaces in my overwriting that reveal what I take to be the university's underlying value system. What an insult upon insults that Columbia thinks we won't closely read. But we do, we will, and we will win.

LIZ BOWEN

MUSIC

"I just wanna con u"

She didn't like

the spiritual equivalent of

my pride I'm doing the best

People

But I am

funny I have

class

Thank you

Thank you

F-ck you You are kitty litter

I'm

taking you down I am a perfect man

I have hurt

the picture this paints is

joy my music my

life

I can be

I am the best man And I

wish people would

say I was like R Kelley

My Music, My Life

I wanted to create an erasure but was overwhelmed by many voices that need manipulating. I say this without hesitation because of how often our voices are manipulated. Then, Ryan Adams. I remembered standing in the stone bleachers at Red Rocks last summer listening to his sad love songs. I went to hear a female-led band, First Aid Kit, who opened, but stayed for songs of his I knew. I love sad songs, especially since my abrupt and emotionally abusive breakup two years ago. I watched all the men in the crowd, singing with their girlfriends, many drunk or stoned, because: Red Rocks. I texted a man from my teens, who I loved, and maybe what I mean is that I wanted him to love me. A man I found myself in bed with, blacked out, post-sex I don't remember agreeing to, ashamed. He loves Ryan Adams. He loves men singing, or rapping, or anything that sounds like men feeling. When I read Ryan Adams's tweets about his divorce from Mandy Moore, how he called her intellectually void, how he lashed out, then made it about him and his mental health, I knew that feeling well. I took every quote I could find and smashed it all together, removed the punctuation, then printed it out and took a child's red unscented Mr. Sketch marker to it until I found truth: me me me. I wanted something cheap, then I wanted black. I found oil pastels, something I feel too void to use correctly, and smeared until what was left was the red and black of rock-and-roll and what men really say when they apologize.

TARA SHEA BURKE

Summer **Love**

Originally Performed by Justin Timberlake

Ridin` in the drop top with the top down
Saw you switchin' lanes girl
Pull up to the red light, lookin' right
Come let me get your name girl
Tell me where you from, what you do, what you like
Let me pick your brain girl
And tell me how they got that pretty little face on that pretty little frame girl
But let me show you 'round, let me take you out
Bet you we could have some fun girl
'Cause we can do it fast (fast), slow, whichever way you wanna run girl
But let me buy you drinks, better yet rings
Do it how you want it done girl
And who would've thought that **you** could be the one 'cause I

I **can**'t wait to fall in love with you
You can't wait to fall in love with me
This just can't be summer love, you'll see
This just can't be summer love (L-O-V-E)

Come on and lemme show you 'round
Let me **take** you out, bet you we could have some fun girl
'Cause we can dress it up, we can dress it down
Any way you want it done girl
Or we can stay home, talkin' on the phone
Rappin' 'til we see the sun girl
Do what I gotta do, just gotta show you that I'm the one girl
Well I'mma freak you right, each and every night
I know how to do it insane girl
'Cause I can make it hot, make it stop
Make you wanna say **my name** girl
Come on baby please 'cause I'm on my knees
Can't get you off my brain girl
But who would've thought that you could be the one **'cause I**

I **can't** wait to fall in love with you
You can't wait to fall in love with me
This just can't be summer love, you'll see
This just can't be summer love (L-O-V-E)

'Cause I can't wait to fall in love with you

You can't wait to fall in love with me
This just can't be summer love, you'll see
This just can't be summer love (L-O-V-E)

The summer's over for the both of us
But that doesn't mean we should **give up on** love
You're the one I've been thinking of
And I knew the day I met you you'd be the one

Oh!I can't wait to fall in love with you
You can't wait to fall in love with **me**
This just can't be summer love, you'll see
This just can't be summer love (L-O-V-E)

'Cause I can't wait to fall in love with you
You can't wait to fall in love with me
This just can't be summer love, you'll see
This just can't be summer love (L-O-V-E)

Pop music is omnipresent—it blasts in lobbies and restaurants, grocery stores and bars. Yet when I actually listen to much of pop music, rather than letting it wash over me as background noise, I notice patriarchal, oppressive messages in the lyrics. Even an innocent-seeming song, like Justin Timberlake's "Summer Love," falters upon closer inspection: it's about a guy hitting on a girl in the car next to him. It's impossible to escape music like this, and I wanted to fight back. When I erased this song, I cut until a female character arose and said her peace. The song title, artist, and the song's lyrics are greyed out but still legible in the text so readers know the words that caused the narrator's anger—or her fear.

TRACY GOLD

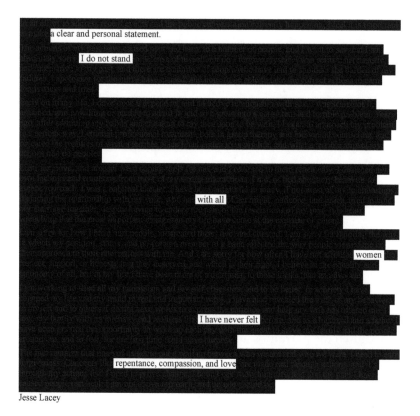
a clear and personal statement.
I do not stand
with all
women
I have never felt
repentance, compassion, and love
Jesse Lacey

"Okay I Believe You, But"

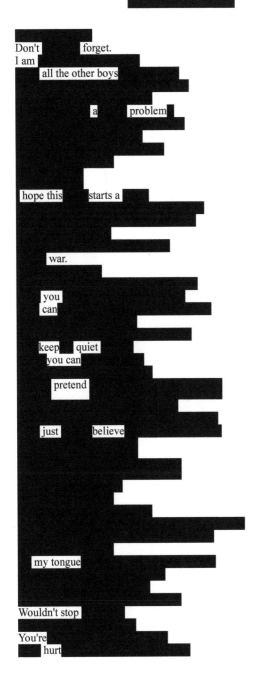

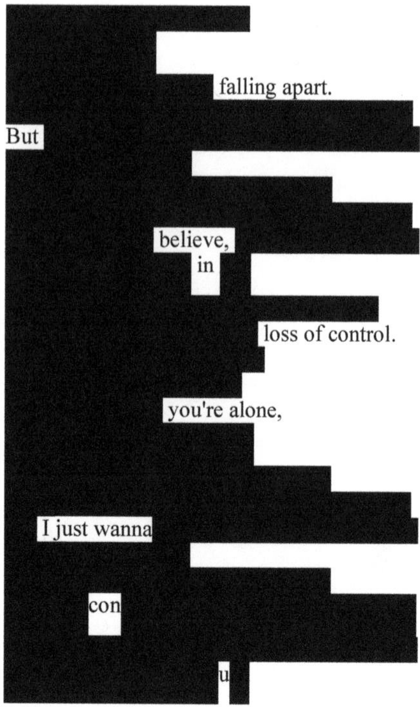
falling apart.
But
believe,
in
loss of control.
you're alone,
I just wanna
con
u

Every aspect of the #MeToo movement hit hard, but it was particularly the news on Brand New's lead singer/writer Jesse Lacey having harassed and groomed a teenager that was really hurtful. As a survivor of assault and an adult who deals with trauma, I often turned towards Brand New's music to cope, and with this news, I felt an isolation and betrayal from my coping mechanisms. The erasures I've completed on Jesse Lacey's admission/PR statement and on Brand New's song "Okay, I Believe You, But My Tommy Gun Don't" helps to highlight the language of denial and victim-blaming that seem to be the epicenter of these songs and responses. Brand New's music has always had a voice that seemed to be exploration of an individual wronged or how others have shaped the singer for the worse. However, unpacking them uncovers that the subject is a man who is blaming women for his own sins. Embedded in these songs/statements are damaging views of women that, once erased, cannot hide the truth of Lacey's actions.

ASH MIRANDA

THE HISTORY OF HIP HOP
ERASUREMIX

1981 – *After Afrika Bambaataa*

Get funky?
Zulu Nation—get funky?
Taste the funk,
get on down.
Bambaataa's funky!
Chase your dreams
up out your body.
Socialize your soul.

It's a dream.

Come play,
you scream.
We know
house of funk,
head   for   disco.

The D.J.
takes you
(poof),
get bump.

Rock rock   don't stop.
Rock rock   don't stop.

Emphasize ego.
People say: "live."
Shucks,
no.
Play is free.
Be,
you be.

Rock rock   don't stop.
Rock rock   don't stop.

You're hot,

nature's children
on Mother Earth,
our rock.
Time has come,
you got soul.
Are you ready?
Hump bump get bump,
let's go.

Twist and turn,
body slide.
You got body,
bounce,
pounce.
Rock it,
don't stop it.
Don't stop
tickin',
tockin',
around the clock.

Keep rockin' and shockin'.
Don't stop it. (Crowd repeats)
Hit me. (Crowd repeats)
Pow Wow. (Crowd repeats)
Force.

You rock it.
It's the century!
Such a melody!
Our world,
a land
of master jam.
Chase your dreams
up out your body.
Socialize your soul.

It's a dream.

Rock it (Crowd repeats)
Shock it (Crowd repeats)
Everybody say (Crowd repeats)
Planet Rock (Crowd repeats)

The sure shot (Crowd repeats)
Planet Rock (Crowd repeats)
The sure shot (Crowd repeats)

Twist and turn
your body.
You got body,
bounce,
pounce.
Hit me,
taste the funk.
Just hit me.
Bambaataa's so funky!

Rate the message,
boys.
Get on it.
Feel the groove.
Ya know,
be cool.
Boogie.
Go down,
low,
to the ground

Everybody,
don't stop it!
Don't stop!
Don't stop it... (Crowd repeats)

I'm fascinated by the poetics of hip hop. I consider hip hop verse to be the most robust and significant American poetic form ever created. When I started working on my series of erasure poems in hip hop, ErasuReMix, I was intrigued by the way hip hop's various poetic elements can be distilled by erasure. In the case of "1981," I sought out to give a platform to the accusations against one of hip hop's most significant pioneers, while preserving the energy of this highly influential poem. For me, the process helped me confront my own complicated relationship to the genre that raised me and also make some space for my own struggles as a survivor of childhood sexual assault.

VICTORIO REYES ASILI

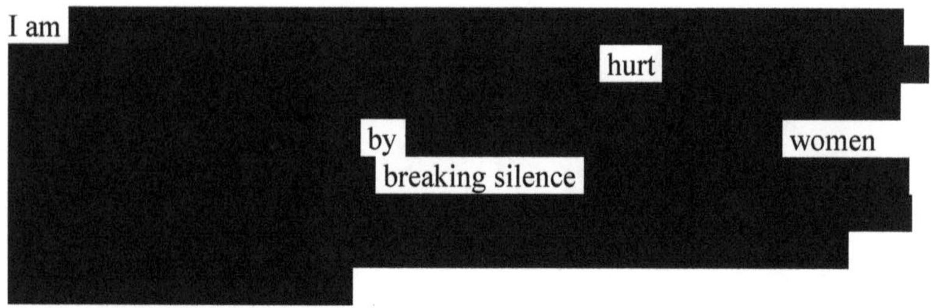
I am
hurt
by
women
breaking silence

I am
never
my behavior

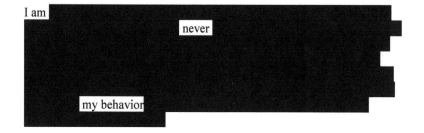

Erasing Matt Mondanile's statement, while it involved placing thick black bars over most of his and his lawyers' clinically selected words, did not make me feel as if I were altering anything. It only illuminated what was truly there when I read his statement; an insulting lack of substance even resembling an apology. I wanted to command attention to what I saw—a hyper-fixation on himself and a negligence to even try and seem accountable. In his statement, he is asking people to believe that his actions did not represent him. As if he and his actions were not one entity. And I, by making these erasures, wanted to present the undeniable truth that we are our actions. And that Matt is his. The way we make people feel is no coincidence; it represents who we are and the mark we leave in our communities.

KIP SHANKS

HOLLYWOOD

"The fact is I am a predator"

I have been a predator — I am a predator

(Microsoft Word Track Changes)

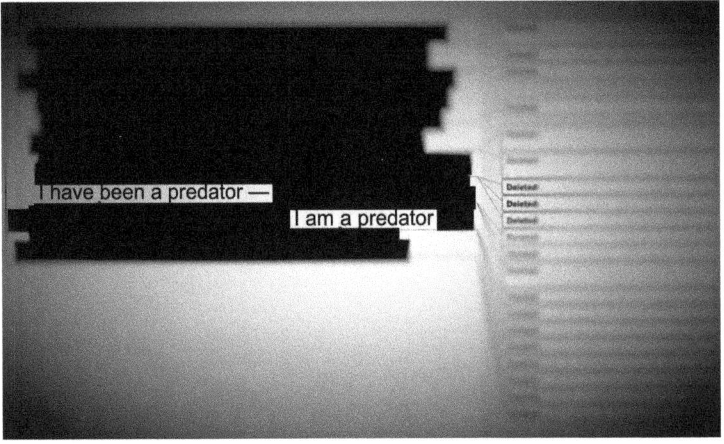

huge ill-tempered predator person
never see deeply aggressive privilege
(Microsoft Word Auto-Summary Cloud)

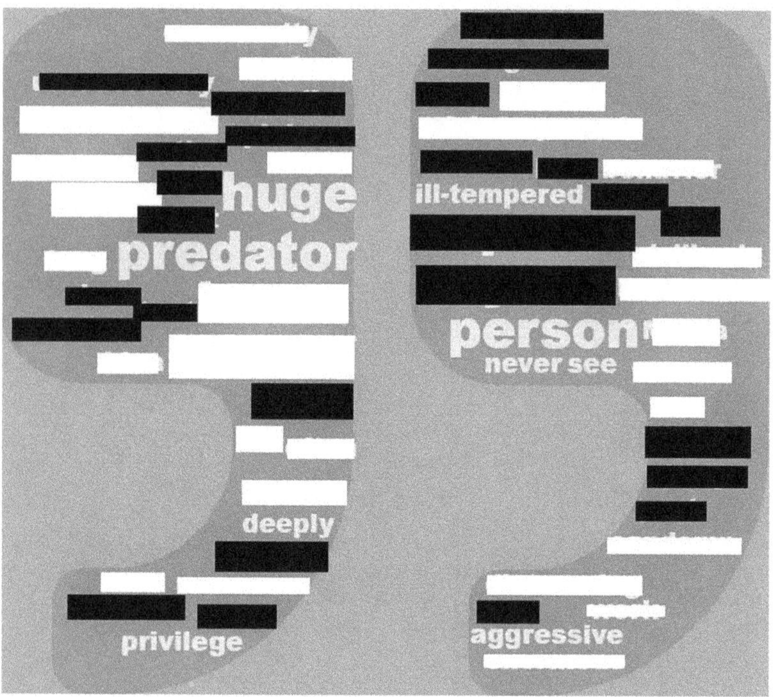

The fact is I am a predator
(iOS Disk Utility)

****

2017-11-16 23:33:46 -0500: Disk Utility started
2017-11-16 23:35:42 -0500: Preparing to securely remove data from disk: "https://www.hollywoodreporter.com/news/transparent-star-alleges-jeffrey-tambor-sexually-harassed-her-got-physical-1059306"
2017-11-16 23:35:42 -0500: DOD Compliant 7-Pass Secure Erase (DOD 5220-22 M)
2017-11-16 23:36:19 -0500: Secure Erase skipped after 18 seconds (0.3% complete)
2017-11-16 23:36:19 -0500: Preparing to erase: "https://www.hollywoodreporter.com/news/transparent-star-alleges-jeffrey-tambor-sexually-harassed-her-got-physical-1059306"
2017-11-16 23:36:19 -0500: Partition Scheme: Master Boot Record (1 volume will be erased)
2017-11-16 23:36:19 -0500: Size: 8.17 GB; File system: MS-DOS (FAT)
2017-11-16 23:36:19 -0500: Unmounting disk
2017-11-16 23:36:19 -0500: Erasing 512 bytes per physical sector, /dev/rdisk5s1: 15933464 sectors in 1991683 FAT32 clusters (4096 bytes/cluster)
~~, I've had the huge privilege — and huge responsibility — of Maura Pfefferman,, in a show that. Now I find myself accused of behavior that any civilized person would condemn unreservedly. N't the easiest person to work with. I can be, and I express my opinions ly But I have never been a predator ever. I am deeply sorry if any action of mine was ever misinterpreted by anyone as being or if I ever offended or hurt anyone. But, for all my flaws, not and the idea that someone might see me in that way is more distressing than I can express.~~
2017-11-16 23:36:23 -0500: Mounting disk
2017-11-16 23:36:25 -0500: Erase complete
For the past four years playing a transgender woman I know has had an enormous, positive impact on a community that has been too long dismissed and misunderstood, I know I have always been volatile and ill-tempered, too often without tact — sexually aggressive. The fact is I am a predator.

****

===== Thursday, November 16, 2017 11:36:25 PM Eastern Standard Time =====

Rather than physical ink to do my striking-through, I opted instead for something almost as quotidian as that big black marker on our desks: the personal computer. Deletion being negation—a deliberate dithering of all things affirmative—to me, digitally erasing Jeffrey Tambor's non-apology made for the most apt annulment.

LOGAN K. YOUNG

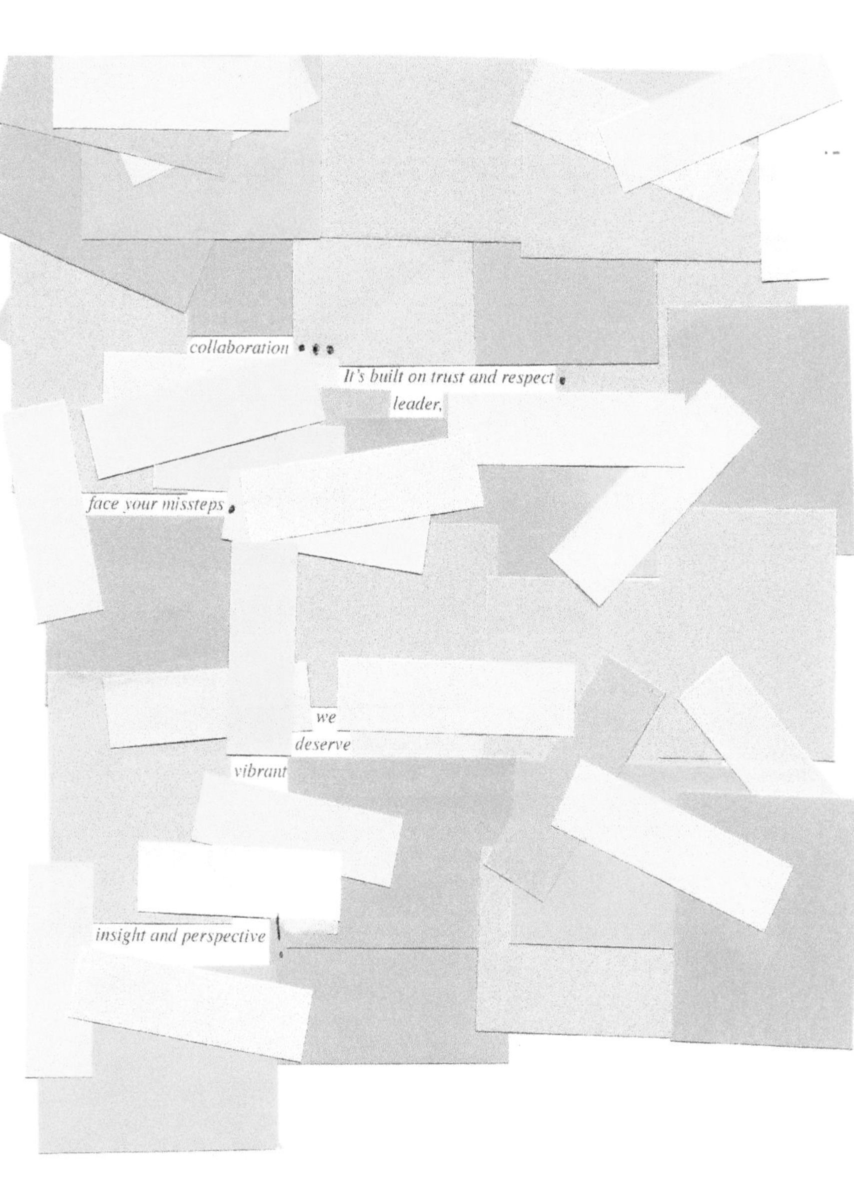
collaboration . . .
It's built on trust and respect .
leader,
face your missteps .
we
deserve
vibrant
insight and perspective !

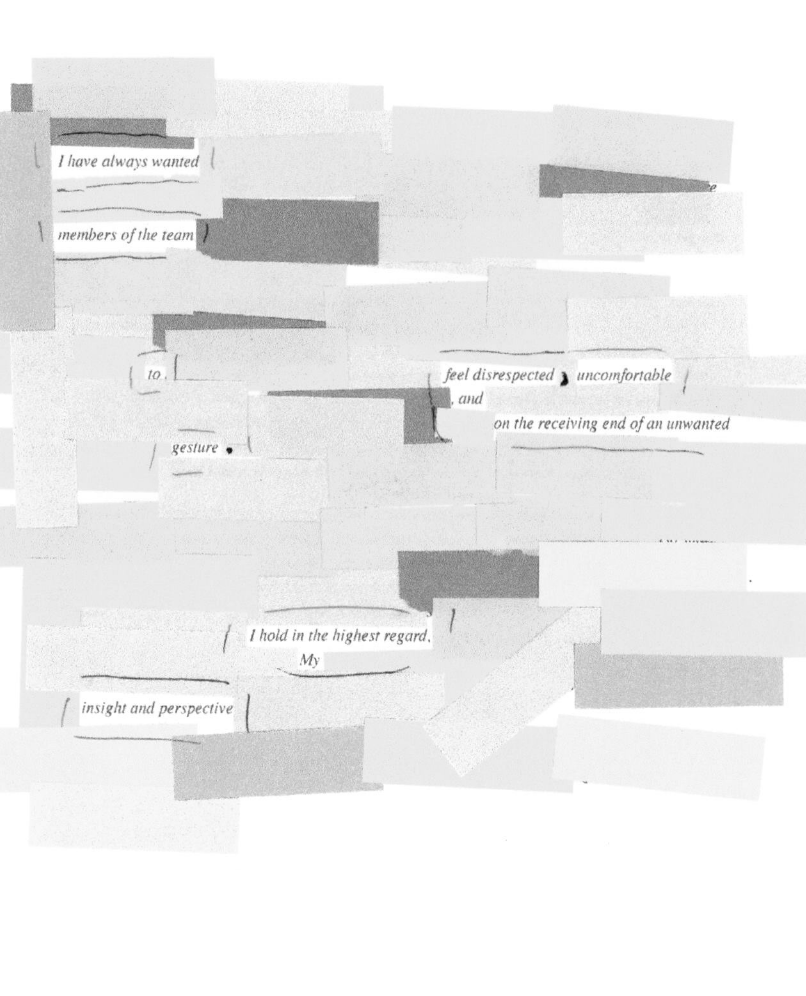
I have always wanted
members of the team
to
feel disrespected, uncomfortable
, and
on the receiving end of an unwanted
gesture.
I hold in the highest regard.
My
insight and perspective

"Setting Fire to Our Demons" and "You're Always So Honest" are both created from the apology memo John Lasseter wrote to the staff of Pixar Animation Studios after sexual harassment allegations and accusations of a toxic work environment. The original memo can be found on Variety.com and many other websites.

In "Setting Fire to Our Demons," I wanted to find a positive message. I hope after readers engage with the poem, they find the courage to take a stand if they feel they've been wronged.

When working on "You're Always So Honest," I felt like there was an underlying message. Unfortunately, I imagine there are some bosses in the world who may align with the words I pulled from the memo.

I erased the original memo using sticky notes.

EMILY WALLING

SPORTS

"I had an unfair advantage"

Lance Armstrong's full statement on USADA
Armstrong does not recognize agency's right to ban him
August 24, 2012, www.cyclingnews.com

every man has to say,
I had an unfair
advantage I
subjected to
my family, and my work
to this nonsense. I
a charade.

If I could confront
the I that is so one-sided and unfair.
. The only physical evidence is the
. I made available
around the world. Whatever
is the point in the end,
?

the
punishing I

the
I stiff-arm
bully, threatening in
its motives

arrogantly
I cheated.
I played ,
the
pervert system
out of spite or for
a sweetheart

I competed against
the strongest man

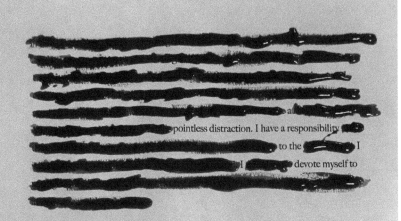

a
pointless distraction. I have a responsibility
to the I
I devote myself to

It's hard to break up with your idols.

Since December 2017, a framed yellow jersey hangs on the kitchen wall. It's the jersey Lance Armstrong wore in his first Tour de France win in 1999. The jersey is bright. The frame overwhelms the wall.

When my partner first decided to ask his mother to buy him this jersey (and have it framed) for a Christmas present, I told him it could not live in the bedroom or my studio. It could not live in those places because my childhood was deeply marred by pathological narcissists and I could not have a relic of one of America's most pathological narcissists occupy a place in which I needed safety from those traumas.

Lance Armstrong is the reason my partner fell in love with the sport of cycling. Although my partner interrogates the narcissism behind Armstrong's fall from grace, he still struggles holding onto his fraudulence against what Armstrong has meant for his relationship to a sport he loves so much.

We'd been together six months when Armstrong interviewed with Oprah and confessed to cheating his way through seven Tour de France titles. We were watching the interview together, but in our separate residences, texting our way through it. My partner was devastated and enraged. These days, however, he fanboys about Lance while I rant my rage in response.

For me, it was never the cheating or the doping. It was the privilege he wielded like a weapon, both on camera and off. It was how easily he could imply women were whores when questioned about his behavior. It was his split from Sheryl Crow after her breast cancer diagnosis. It was how ruthlessly he threw whomever he could find under the bus whenever he was in the hot seat. It was that glint in his eye, the dull stare, of a person who believes the world is for him to take, in whatever way he chooses.

I redacted Armstrong's words with these things in mind, at the table, with his yellow jersey hovering over me, refracting the sunlight. I used fake blood to erase the spin that surrounded his statement, just like the blood he pretended to have. Just like he did in a van, hiding in plain sight, I bled out the words of his self-victimization, and left his fixation on his own I, a fixation leaving many victims in its wake.

ADDIE TSAI

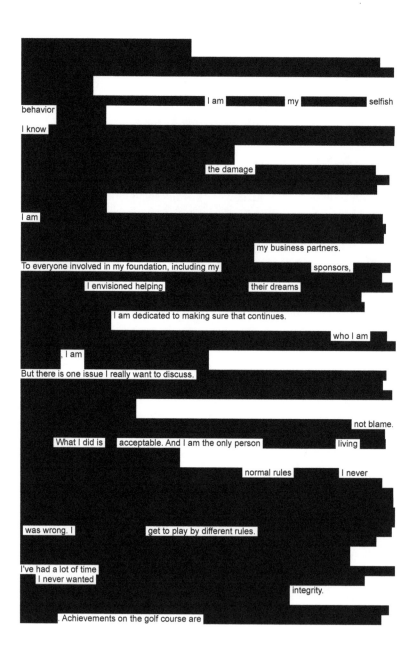
I am
my
selfish
behavior
I know
the damage
I am
my business partners.
To everyone involved in my foundation, including my
sponsors,
I envisioned helping
their dreams
I am dedicated to making sure that continues.
who I am
, I am
But there is one issue I really want to discuss.
not blame.
What I did is
acceptable. And I am the only person
living
normal rules
I never
was wrong. I
get to play by different rules.
I've had a lot of time
I never wanted
integrity.
. Achievements on the golf course are

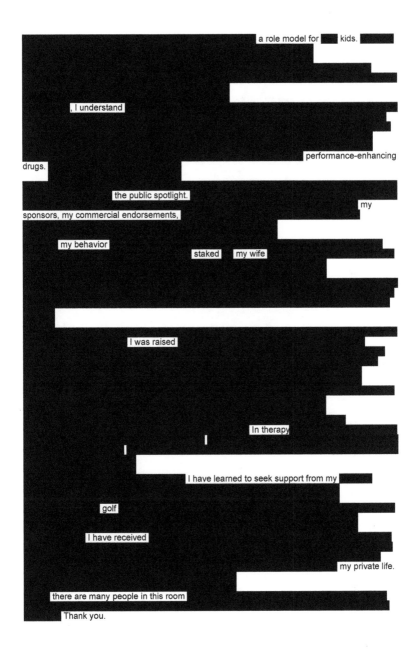
a role model for kids.
, I understand
performance-enhancing
drugs.
the public spotlight.
my
sponsors, my commercial endorsements,
my behavior
staked
my wife
I was raised
In therapy
I
I
I have learned to seek support from my
golf
I have received
my private life.
there are many people in this room
Thank you.

Men only apologise when they get caught. When they get caught, they apologise. The apology is to protect their income, to protect the sponsors, themselves, no one else. The apology is as self-serving as the action they committed.

SHANE JESSE CHRISTMASS

LITERATURE

"fuck tender beauty"

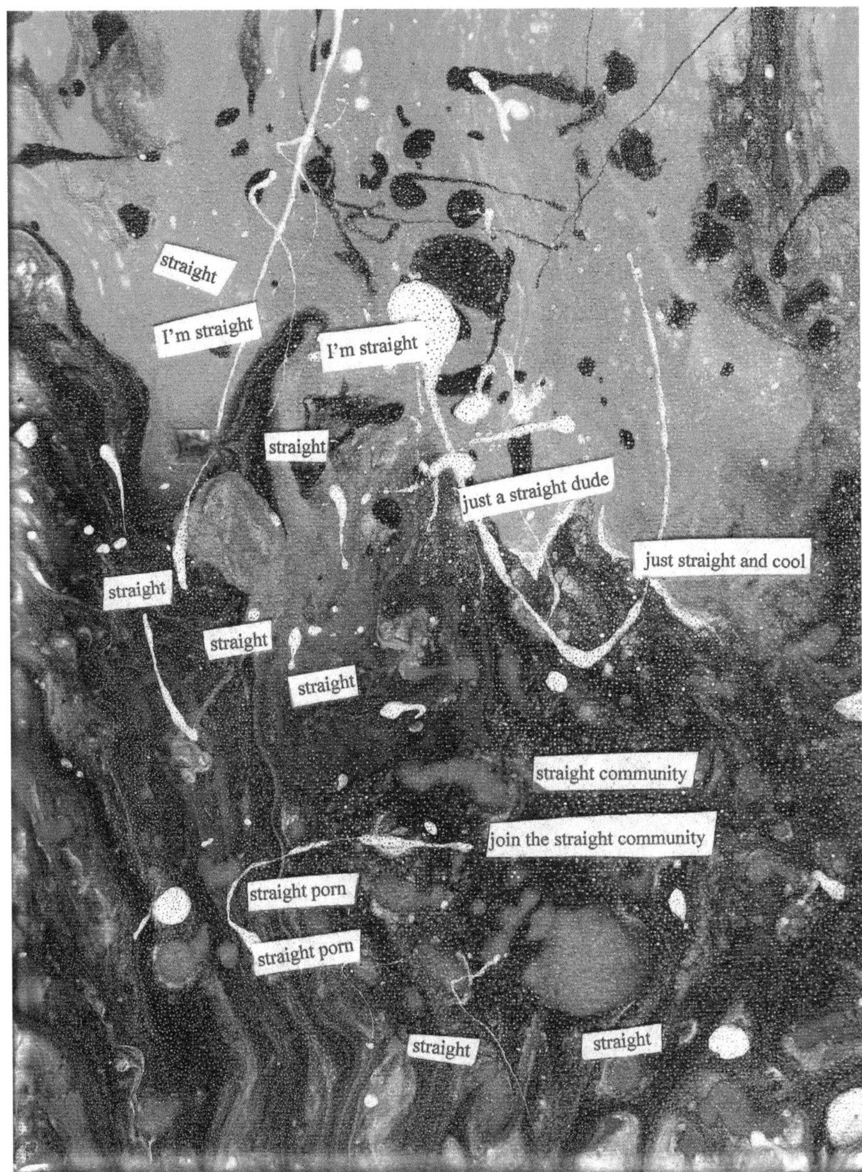
straight
I'm straight
I'm straight
straight
just a straight dude
just straight and cool
straight
straight
straight
straight community
join the straight community
straight porn
straight porn
straight
straight

This poem is meant to point out James Franco's appropriation of queer stories for his own gain. It emphasizes his hypocrisy by pulling every time he uses the word "straight" in his poem. I used every color in the rainbow for paint but when placed out of order and used improperly they become muddied and dull. Franco's recent alleged inappropriate sexual behavior towards women came to light after making this piece. This piece does not speak to that directly, but the impact of this piece does change.

ALEX VIGUE

MMMMMMMMMM

her death

MMMMMM

her

sex.

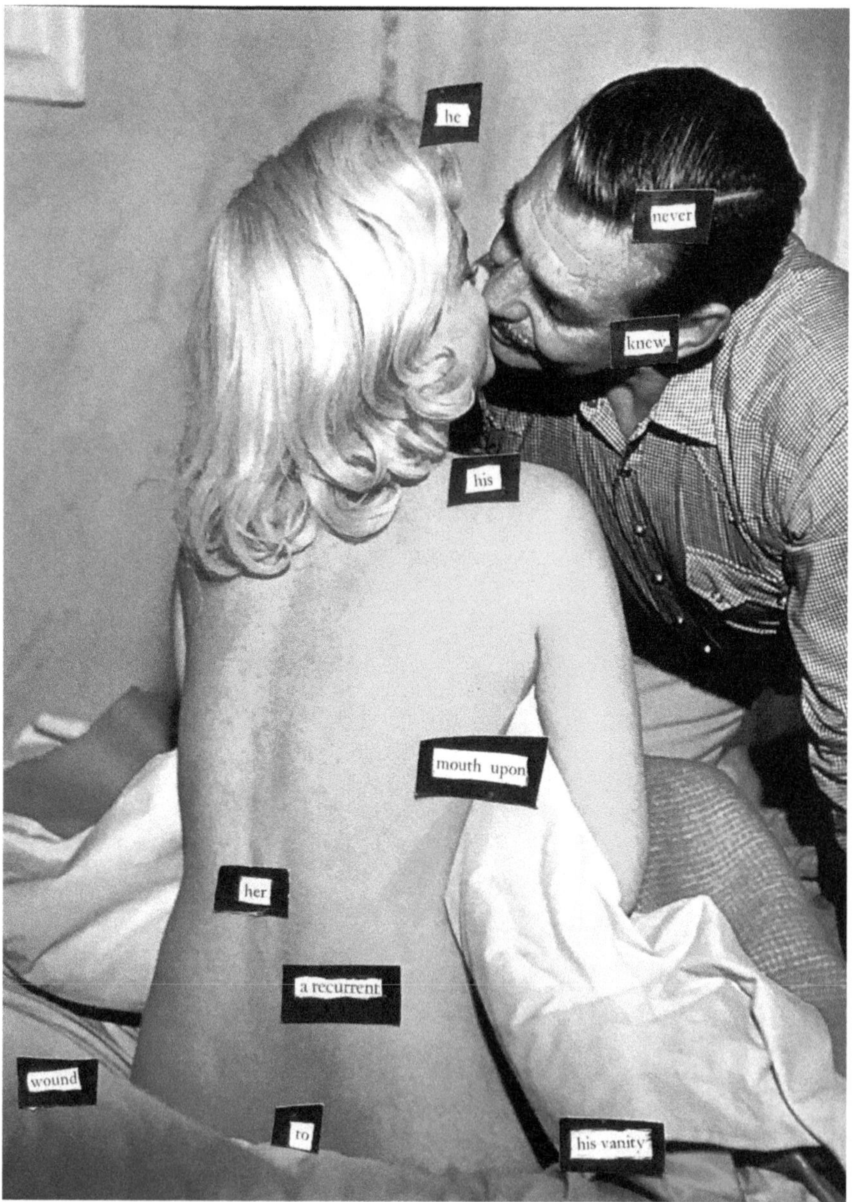
he
never
knew
his
mouth upon
her
a recurrent
wound
to
his vanity

fuck

tender beauty

no
No
never
no
no
not
no
TON SET
no
no
no
no
nothing
no
No
no

trapped in
the myth
the
creation
the
belly
of
Marilyn
Monroe.

While working on my chapbook, *rebel/blonde,* I did a lot of reading and research on Marilyn Monroe. One of the books that I came across at that time was Norman Mailer's biography on Monroe, simply titled *Marilyn.* From the first page, when in the same paragraph Mailer refers to Marilyn as both "the sweet angel of sex," and "a very Stradivarius of sex" I knew I was going to loathe both Mailer and the book. I wasn't wrong.

About a year later, inspired by the erasures of Isobel O'Hare and jay dodd, and considering the broader possibilities of erasure poetry, Mailer's book came back to mind.

I have to admit I didn't go in with a fixed idea as to how I was going to approach the project as a whole, and as such, when I look at the completed erasures now, I see how the voice shifted in the process of making them, as did the style.

The first erasure I did was naturally in the traditional black-out style, only leaving three words left unredacted: "fuck tender beauty." Here, I wasn't trying to reveal a secret message obscured by the surrounding text, but instead wanted to create a visually bold rebuke in my own voice. A rebuke against Mailer, and by extension, the entire patriarchal hierarchy. Against the idolization of the sweet, innocent, submissive woman, so desirable because she does not talk back.

"MMMMMM her sex" on the other hand, cut to the underlying subtext, one that was not so hidden beneath the surface. Interested in experimenting with the effects of different materials, I switched from black to purple paint, and decided to further adorn the page with tiny gold glitter stars. My hope was that the "prettiness" of it would enhance the irony of the words that remained.

The others all make use of photographs that were included in the book. I found the photograph used in "No" to be particularly provocative in its refusal to play along, and for the first time in these erasures, the speaker becomes Marilyn herself. In the photograph, she is denying the photographer her face, us the gratification of her image, and (in my mind) Mailer her consent. With the tiny refusals encrusted on the pink chiffon over lace, it becomes a very literal protest against the male gaze.

When I started this project, I think I had a grand ambition to make an erasure out of all 262 pages in the book. As of now, I have only done a few more beyond what is represented in this book. I'm not sure how or if I will continue with it, or leave it as it is, but I am very grateful these pieces have found a home in this anthology, edited by the person who inspired them.

MEGHANN BOLTZ

Phyllis Schlafly, "What's Wrong with 'Equal Rights' for Women?" (1972)

Of all the classes of people who ever lived, the American woman is the most privileged. We have the most rights and rewards, and the fewest duties. Our unique status is the result of a fortunate combination of circumstances.

1. We have the immense good fortune to live in a civilization which respects the family as the basic unit of society. This respect is part and parcel of our laws and our customs. It is based on the fact of life—which no legislation or agitation can erase—that women have babies and men don't.

If you don't like this fundamental difference, you will have to take up your complaint with God because He created us this way. The fact that women, not men, have babies is not the fault of selfish and domineering men, or of the establishment, or of any clique of conspirators who want to oppress women. It's simply the way God made us.

Our Judeo-Christian civilization has developed the law and custom that, since women must bear the physical consequences of the sex act, men must be required to bear the other consequences and pay in other ways. These laws and customs decree that a man must carry his share by physical protection and financial support of his children and of the woman who bears his children, and also by a code of behavior which benefits and protects both the woman and the children.

THE GREATEST ACHIEVEMENT OF WOMEN'S RIGHTS

This is accomplished by the institution of the family. Our respect for the family as the basic unit of society, which is ingrained in the laws and customs of our Judeo-Christian civilization, is the greatest single achievement in the entire history of women's rights. It assures a woman the most precious and important right of all—the right to keep her own baby and to be supported and protected in the enjoyment of watching her baby grow and develop.

The institution of the family is advantageous for women for many reasons. After all, what do we want out of life? To love and be loved? Mankind has not discovered a better nest for a lifetime of reciprocal love. A sense of achievement? A man may search 30 to 40 years for accomplishment in his profession. A woman can enjoy real achievement when she is young—by having a baby. She can have the satisfaction of doing a job well—and being recognized for it. Do we want financial security? We are fortunate to have the great legacy of Moses, the Ten Commandments, especially this one: "Honor thy father and thy mother that thy days may be long upon the land." Children are a woman's best social security—her best guarantee of social benefits such as old age pension, unemployment compensation, workman's compensation, and sick leave. The family gives a woman the physical, financial and emotional security of the home—for all her life.

THE FINANCIAL BENEFITS OF CHIVALRY

2. The second reason why American women are a privileged group is that we are the beneficiaries of a tradition of special respect for women which dates from the Christian Age of Chivalry. The honor and respect paid to Mary, the Mother of Christ, resulted in all women, in effect, being put on a pedestal. This respect for women is not just the lip service that politicians pay to "God, Motherhood, and the Flag." It is not—as some youthful agitators seem to think—just a matter of opening doors for women, seeing that they are seated first, carrying their bundles, and helping them in and out of automobiles. Such good manners are merely the superficial evidences of a total attitude toward women which expresses itself in many more tangible ways, such as money. In other civilizations, such as the African and the American Indian, the men strut around wearing feathers and beads and hunting and fishing (great sport for men!), while the women do all the hard, tiresome drudgery including the tilling of the soil (if any is done), the hewing of wood, the making of fires, the carrying of water, as well as the cooking, sewing and caring for babies. This is not the American way because we were lucky enough to inherit the traditions of the Age of Chivalry. In America, a man's first significant purchase is a diamond for his bride, and the largest financial investment of his life is a home for her to live in. American husbands work hours of overtime to buy a fur piece or other finery to keep their wives in fashion, and to pay premiums on their life insurance policies to provide for her comfort when she is a widow (benefits in which he can never share). In the states which follow the English common law, a wife has a dower right in her husband's real estate which he cannot take away from her during life or by his will. A man cannot dispose of his real estate without his wife's signature. Any sale is subject to her 1/3 interest. Women fare even better in the states which follow the Spanish and French community- property laws, such as California, Arizona, Texas and

I wanted to examine statements by women who have a stake in upholding patriarchal structures. I had never heard of Phyllis Schlafly or the Equal Rights Amendment until my early twenties, when I worked for a multi-millionaire husband-and-wife couple at a tech company. The wife told me that Schlafly made some good points about how business owners could get backed into a corner if men and women were treated equally, which made me make a face. In this 1972 speech, Schlafly employs double standards for men depending on which freedoms their wives are allowed. Men are fiscally responsible, loving, chivalrous husbands who earn all of the money to take care of their wives, who do all of the housework—but in Illinois, where "real-estate dower laws were repealed...a husband can now sell the family home, spend the money on his girlfriend or gamble it away, and his faithful wife of 30 years can no longer stop him." Men are morally pure protectors except in Illinois, where the law allows them not to be? (I also can't believe the statement about how un-American American Indians are, or how her "American women" umbrella term apparently doesn't include any women of color, or women whose financial realities require their participation in the labor force.) My personal belief is that many traditional-gender-role champions who think of (chaste, white) women as a sacred, protected class built for mothering are actually mystified and disgusted by cis women's bodies...which is why I erased this speech in menstrual blood.

SARAH LYN ROGERS

my

sex
is

the most
astonishing
collection
of

people.

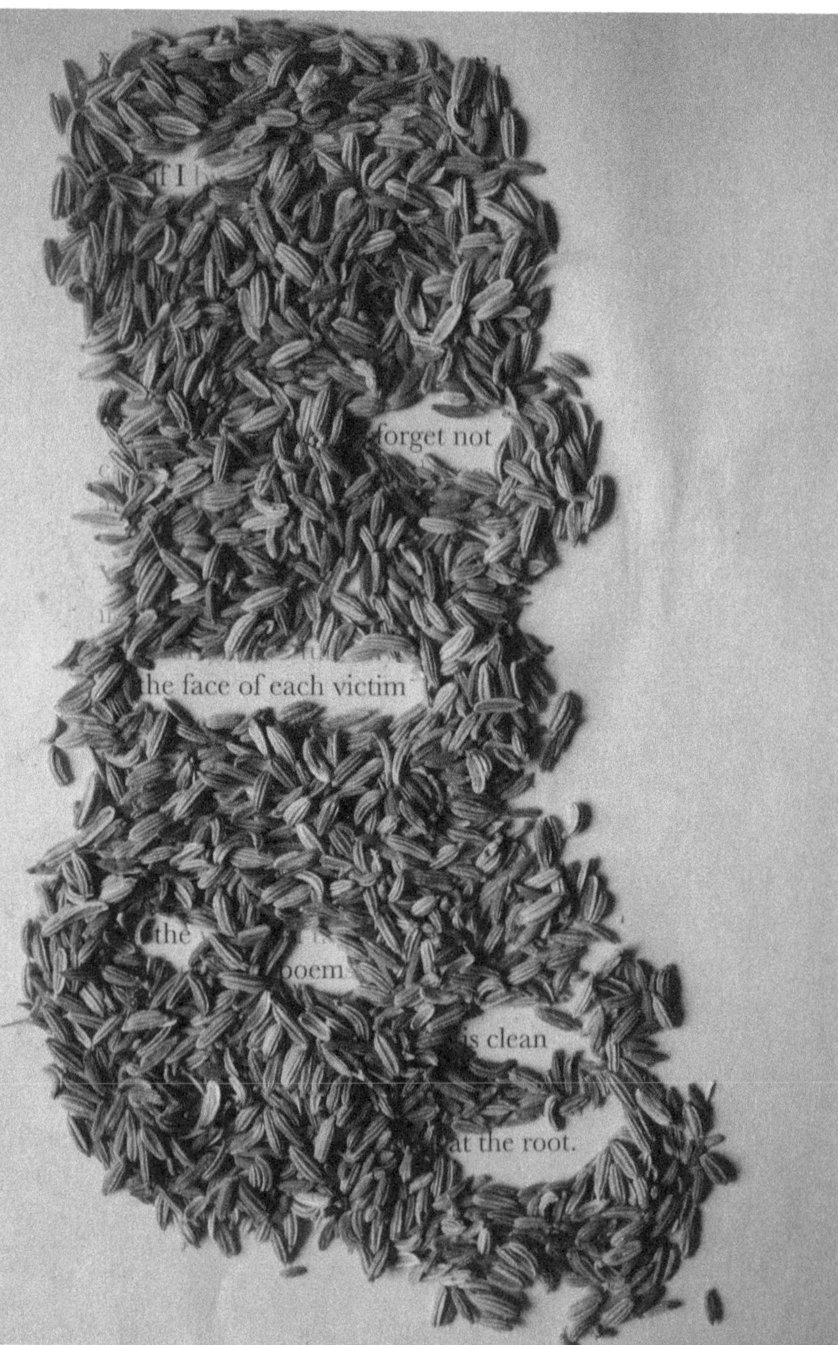
forget not
the face of each victim
the
poem
is clean
at the root.

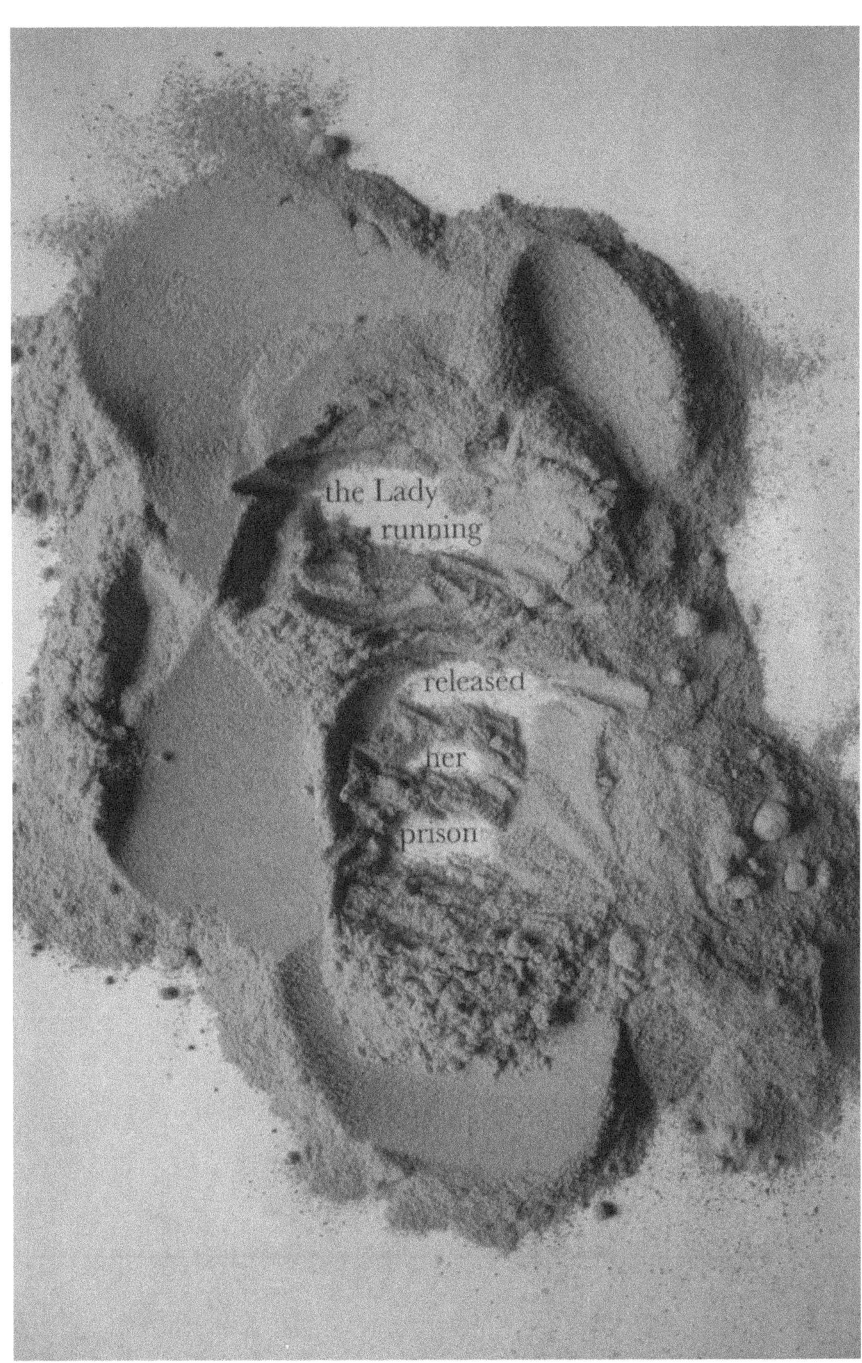
the Lady
running
released
her
prison

I know
to be like bones.
But I want
to be
the sun.

We live in a world filled with

cities filled with

prisons

What a world

that

failed

to feel their hurt.

When I first heard the call for erasures of misogynistic work, I thumbed through my bookshelf and found Norman Mailer's *Modest Gifts*, a collection of his poems and drawings that someone had left at my place. Often in a sarcastic and cynical voice, Mailer's poems belittle the queer and female body ("did your little womb go pitty pat pat" was one line I crossed out) and explore the violence of his experience at war without much generosity toward the other side. I chose his text to erase because I want more joy in poetry; I want people to be unfurling and celebrated, to lean toward wonder instead of ridicule.

I don't draw or paint, so most of my erasures consist of Sharpie on paper, but Mailer's drab cynicism still lingered in this format. I do cook—and aren't the best meals ones that are colorful? And don't the best connections happen over shared meals? I pulled out spices and began playing, making poems of sugar, fennel, turmeric, red pepper flakes, and coffee grounds, a "meal" now shared with you. Perhaps if Mailer had sat down at a few more of our tables, he would have seen us with all the delight that we are.

ABIGAIL ZIMMER

"" He bellows, . " I'll be back. stay right here "

""

" I'll return. ."

His footsteps fade

She watched him until he was gone. . She worked with a numbness she caught herself singing

She held her breath .

.

At any moment it might happen.

a thunderstorm the faintest pressure of the atmosphere the shifts and shadows and vapors suspended in the waiting time of the coming storm. The caged flowers blew sighs of warning. "Time, time, time, time ..."

And then the engulfments of , shutting in, forever.

any instant there would be a silence, footsteps on the path, , and her *running* to answer....

. Why ?

And then it happened.

, she flung wide a door. But by this time there was nothing.

she stopped herself. She was supposed to go nowhere. The doctor would be angry if she ran off.

Ylla

He bellows, "I'll be back.
stay right here.

I'll return."
His footsteps fade
She watched him until he was gone.

She worked with a numbness
she caught herself singing.

She held her breath.

At any moment it might happen.
a thunderstorm
the faintest pressure of the atmosphere
the shifts and shadows and vapors
suspended in the waiting time of the coming storm.

The caged flowers blew sighs of warning.
Time, time, time, time …
And then the engulfments of shutting in, forever.

any instant there would be a silence,
footsteps on the path, and her *running* to answer …
Why?
And then it happened.

she flung wide a door. But by this time
there was nothing.
she stopped herself. She was supposed to go nowhere.
The doctor would be angry if she ran off.

all of you were dead, all but a few. You're rare, don't you *know* that?"

"That's not true."

". I saw the bodies. . Thousands of them."

"That's ridiculous. We're *alive!*"

", you're invaded, "

Don't you see the city there?"

. "Why, that city's been dead thousands of years."

"Dead. I slept there yesterday!"

"It's dead."

"It's alive! There are women with flowers in their hands.

, that city is Green ; that's the new Highway. You're mixed up.

There See?"

"No."

Night Meeting

"all of you were dead, all but a few. You're rare, don't you *know* that?"
"That's not true."
"I saw the bodies. Thousands of them."
"That's ridiculous. We're *alive!*"
"you're invaded."
"Don't you see the city there?"
"Why, that city's been dead thousands of years."
"Dead. I slept there yesterday!"

"It's dead."
"It's alive! There are women with flowers
in their hands. that city is Green; that's the new
Highway. You're mixed up.

There.
See?"
"No."

I was awestruck when I saw Ray Bradbury speak in person because he was an amazing orator who talked about writing like I thought about writing. Years later, when I read some of his short story collections, I was shocked at how this well-known science fiction writer treated the women in his stories as melodramatic and flat representations of my gender. When I decided to erase *The Martian Chronicles*, I found an undercurrent of violent images directed toward women and a white-savior complex when it came to Bradbury's supposed criticism of manifest destiny.

RACHEL ANNA NEFF

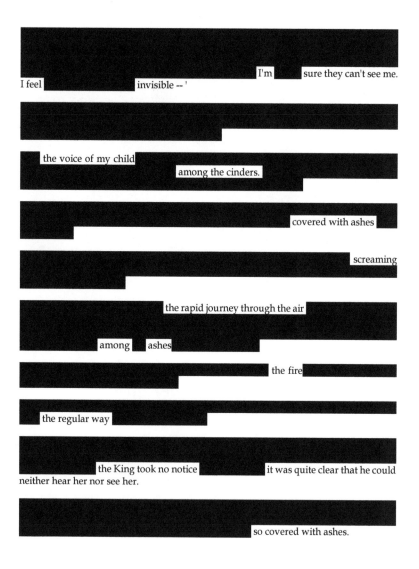

I'm sure they can't see me.
I feel invisible -- '

the voice of my child
among the cinders.

covered with ashes

screaming

the rapid journey through the air
among ashes

the fire

the regular way

the King took no notice it was quite clear that he could
neither hear her nor see her.

so covered with ashes.

I think for a lot of marginalized groups, including women, feeling invisible is a common experience. Especially if we consider how visible we may feel to those in power making the decisions that impact our lives, and how this is "the regular way" of things—fully normalized. The presence of the child reinforces how cyclical this invisibility can be. The king can't see the poem's speaker, can't see her daughter who has become covered in ashes. He takes no notice because he has no reason to notice. Lewis Carroll is a difficult figure, of course, given the suspicions around his relationship with Alice Liddell. However, regardless of why he was interested in photographing that girl so much, my question for him would be, "Did you ever really see her?"

KI RUSSELL

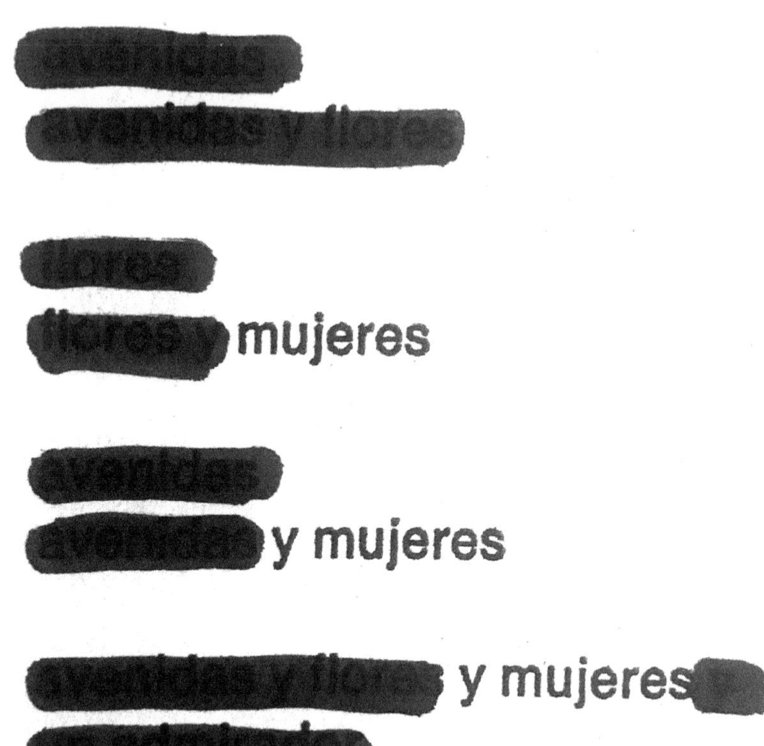

mujeres
y mujeres
y mujeres

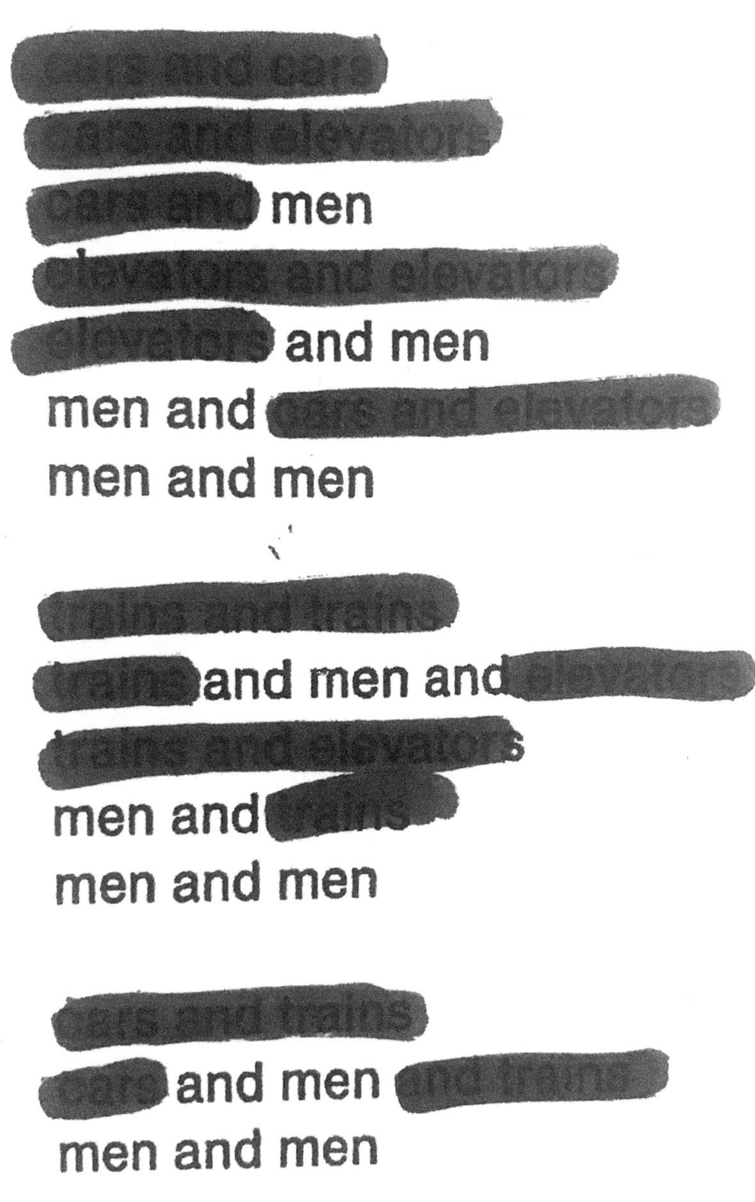

men
and men
men and
men and men

and men and
men and
men and men

and men
men and men

men and men

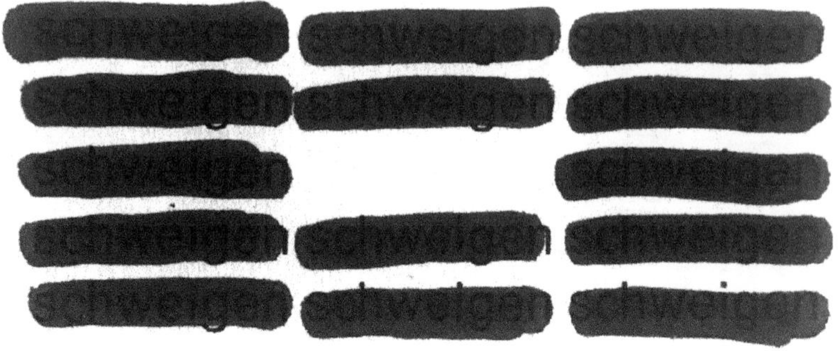
schweigen schweigen schweigen
schweigen schweigen schweigen
schweigen schweigen
schweigen schweigen schweigen
schweigen schweigen schweigen

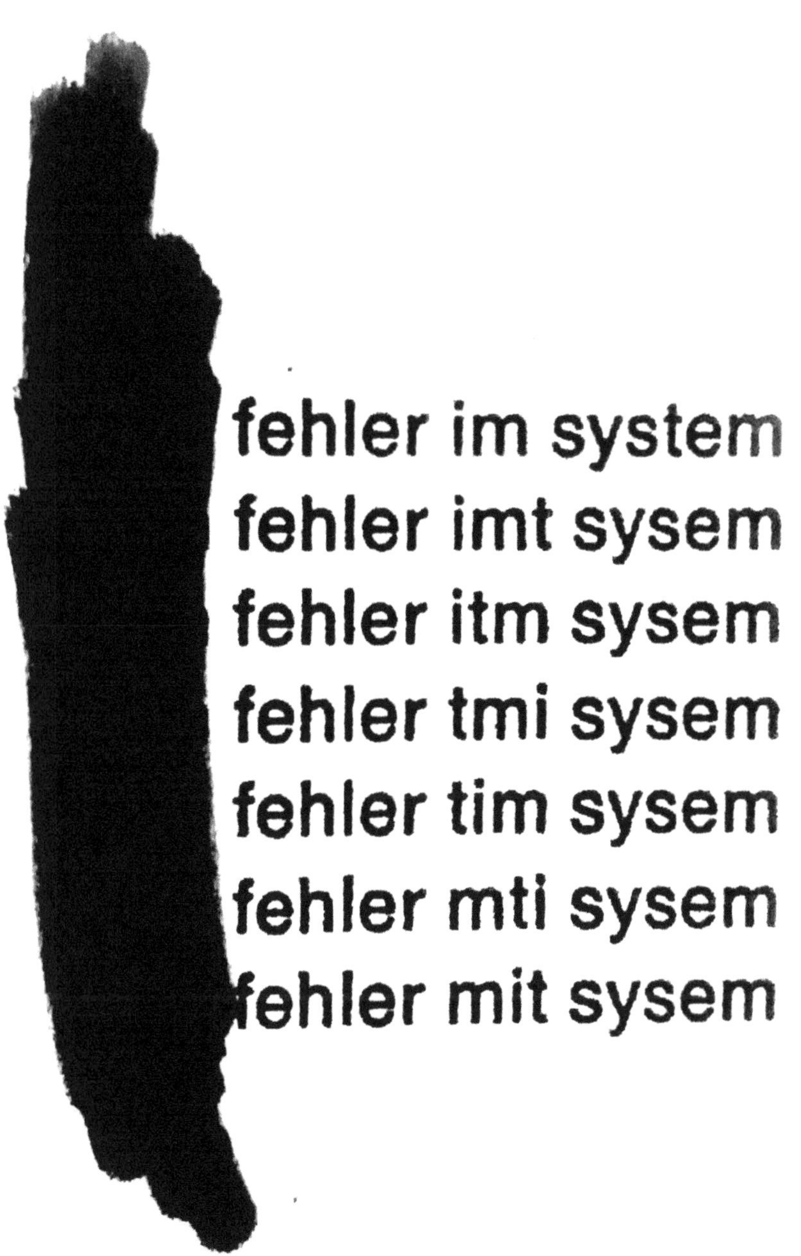
fehler im system
fehler imt sysem
fehler itm sysem
fehler tmi sysem
fehler tim sysem
fehler mti sysem
fehler mit sysem

dein schweigen
mein gedicht

The artist Eugen Gomringer's poem "Avenidas" (1953) sparked a nationwide debate in Germany on sexism and art censorship in 2016. The controversy ignited when the poem, which is featured prominently on the façade of a university building, was called out for being perceived as misogynistic. Specifically, advocates of the #MeToo movement found reprehensible Gomringer's invocation of women's bodies and alleyways. In January 2018, the debate came to a close with what has been called a *Säuberung* [sanitization] of the façade.

The controversy reached a fever pitch in 2017 while I researched Gomringer's oeuvre. I feel this was a fortunate coincidence. I interviewed Gomringer's daughter Nora about her thoughts on the issue. At the Berlin Poetry Festival, I served as personal assistant to Eugen and his lovely wife Nortrud. We discussed the controversy at length. One gloomy afternoon, we drove to the institution and took pictures of the poet standing defiantly with his poem before it was painted over. Admiration and adoration competed with my own feminist inclinations and the importance of feminist readings in art and art criticism.

"Avenidas" is clever. The reader is made to relate to the *admirador*. Both are engaged in the act of looking. Both are playing the role of admiring spectator. Certainly, Gomringer hoped his readers would find pleasure looking at this first example of a new poetic form. But if the reader is to identify with the male gaze, is a heteronormative audience to be assumed as well? My project seeks to draw attention to how the poem's heteronormativity might be indexical of how concrete poetry has—and continues to be—a male-dominated genre.

MAGGIE ROSENAU

FIRST MANIFESTO OF SURREALISM 1924[016]

BY[FOR] ANDRE BRETON

PREFACE

I.

Such is the belief in life, in the most precarious aspects of life, by which is meant real life, that in the end belief is lost. Man, that inveterate dreamer, more and more discontented day by day with his fate, orbits with difficulty around the objects he has been led to make use of, those which indifference has handed him, or his own efforts, almost always his efforts, since he has consented to labour, at least he has not been averse to chancing his luck (what he calls his luck!). A vast modesty is now his lot: he knows what women he has had, what foolish affairs he has been involved in; riches or poverty are nothing to him, he remains in this respect a new-born babe, and as for the consent of his moral conscience, I admit that he does very well without it. If he retains any degree of lucidity, he can do no more than turn to his childhood, which ruined as it has been by his teachers' pains, seems to him nonetheless full of charm. There, the absence of all familiar constraint, furnishes him with a perspective of several lives lived simultaneously; he becomes rooted in this illusion; he no longer wishes to know anything beyond the momentary and extreme facility of everything. Each morning, children set off without concern. Everything is near, the worst material circumstances are fine. The woods are black or white, one will never need to sleep again.

But it is true we would never dare venture so far, it is not merely a question of distance. Menace accumulates, one yields, one abandons a part of the terrain to be conquered. That same imagination that knows no limits, is never permitted to be exercised except according to arbitrary laws of utility; it is incapable of assuming this inferior role for long, and at about the age of twenty, prefers, in general, to abandon Man to his unilluminated destiny.

Let him try, later, now and then, to collect himself, having felt himself little by little losing all reason to live, incapable as he has become of rising to the heights of an exceptional situation such as love, and he will hardly succeed. That is because, from now on, he belongs body and soul to an imperious practical necessity, of which one must never lose sight. His gestures will lose all their expansiveness, his ideas all their grandeur. In what happens to him or might happen, he will perceive only what relates such events to a host of similar events, events in which he has not taken part, waste events. Rather, he will assess them with regard to some one of those events, more reassuring in its outcome than the rest. On no account, will he consider them as offering him salvation.

Dear imagination, what I love most about you, is your unforgiving nature.

The only mark of freedom is whatever still exalts me. I believe it right to maintain forever, our oldest human fanaticism. Indeed that reflects my sole legitimate aspiration. Amidst all the shame we are heir to, it is well to recognize that the widest freedom of spirit remains to us. It is up to us not to abuse it in any serious manner. To make a slave of the imagination, even though what is vulgarly called happiness is at stake, is to fail profoundly to do justice to one's deepest self. Only imagination realises the possible in me, and it is enough to lift for a moment the dreadful proscription; enough also for me to abandon myself to it, without fear of error (as if one could be any more in error). Where does error begin, and security end for the spirit? Is not the possibility of error, for the spirit, rather a circumstance conducive to its well-being?

Madness remains, 'the madness one locks away' as has been so aptly said. That madness or another...Everyone knows, in fact, that the mad owe their incarceration to a number of legally reprehensible actions, and that were it not for those actions, their liberty (or what we see as their liberty) would not be at risk. They may be, in some measure, victims of their imagination, I am prepared to concede that, in the way that it induces them not to observe certain rules, without which the species feels threatened, which it pays us all to be aware of. But the profound indifference they show for the judgment we pass on them, and even the various punishments inflicted on them, allows us to suppose that they derive great solace from imagination, that they enjoy their delirium enough to endure the fact that it is only of value to themselves. And, indeed, hallucinations, illusions etc. are no slight source of pleasure. The most well-ordered sensuality partakes of it, and I know there are many evenings when I would gladly tame that pretty hand which in the last pages of Taine's *L'Intelligence*, indulges in some curious misdeeds. The confidences of the mad, I could pass my whole life inspiring them. They are a scrupulously honest tribe, whose innocence has no peer but my own. Columbus ought to have taken madmen with him to discover America. And see how that folly has gained substance, and endured.

II.

It is not the fear of foolishness that compels us to leave the banner of imagination furled.

The case against the realist position needs to be considered, after considering the materialist position. The latter, more poetic however than the former, admittedly implies on the part of a Man, a monstrous pride, but not a new and more complete degeneration. It should be seen, above all, as a welcome reaction against certain ridiculous spiritualist tendencies. Ultimately, it is not incompatible with a certain nobility of thought.

The realistic position, in contrast, inspired by positivism, from Thomas Aquinas to Anatole France, appears to me to be totally hostile to all intellectual and moral progress. It horrifies me, since it arises from mediocrity, hatred and dull conceit. It is what engenders all the ridiculous books, and insulting plays of our day. It feeds on newspaper articles, and holds back science and art, while applying itself to flattering the lowest tastes of its readers: clarity bordering on stupidity, the life lived by dogs. The activity of the best minds is affected by it, the law of the lowest common denominator imposes itself on them, in the end, as on the others. One amusing result of this state of things, in literature for example, is the vast quantity of novels. Each brings its little measure of 'observation'. Feeling in need of a purge, Paul Valéry recently suggested the compilation of an anthology of as great a number as possible of opening passages from novels, hoping much from the ensuing bouts of insanity. The most famous of authors would be included. Such an idea reflects honour on Paul Valéry who, some time ago, on the subject of novels, assured me that, as far as he was concerned, he would continue to refrain from writing: The Marquise went out at five. But has he kept his word?

III.

If the declarative style, pure and simple, of which the sentence just offered is an example, is almost the rule in novels, it is because, as one must recognise, the authors' ambition is quite limited. The circumstantial, needlessly specific, nature of their respective writings, leads me to think they are amusing themselves at my expense. They spare me not a single one of their issues of characterisation: will he be fair-haired, what will he be called, will we encounter him in summer? So many questions, resolved once and for all, haphazardly; the only power of choice I am left with is to close the book, which I take care to do at about the first page. And the descriptions! Nothing can be compared to their vacuity; it is nothing but the superimposition of images from a catalogue, the author employs them more and more readily, he seizes the opportunity to slip me postcards, he tries to make me fall in step with him in public places:

'The small room into which the young man was shown was decorated with yellow wallpaper: there were geraniums and muslin curtains in the windows; the setting sun cast a harsh light over all…There was nothing special about the chamber. The furniture, of yellow wood, was all quite old. A sofa with a tall curved back, an oval table opposite the sofa, a dressing table and mirror set against the overmantel, chairs against the walls, two or three etchings of little value, representing German girls holding birds in their hands – amounted to all the furniture.' (*Dostoevsky, Crime and Punishment*)

I am in no mood to admit, even for a moment, that the mind welcomes such motifs. It may be argued that this childish description has its place, and that at this point in the novel the author has his reasons for burdening me with it, but he is wasting his time since I avoid entering his room. The idleness, the fatigue of others does not interest me. I have too fragile a notion of life's continuity to equate my moments of depression and weakness with my best. I prefer one to be **silent**, when one ceases to feel. Understand that I am not condemning lack of originality for its lack of originality. I simply say that I take no notice of the empty hours of life, and that it may be an unworthy action for any man to crystallise out those which seem so to him. Allow me to ignore that description of a room, along with a host of others.

Whoa, I'm into psychology, a subject about which I'll take care not to jest.

When first studying art history, my courses only covered the work of men. I leaned toward surrealism, and of course, there was the fur-covered teacup, but other than that, I couldn't name a single piece of surrealist art by a woman. I eventually discovered a rich history of women working in surrealism, and I learned that André Breton was a misogynist. So, I decided to erase his words.

STACEY BALKUN

This is Just
[For Marcia Nardi]

I have eaten

you

so
and so

As a Cloud

[For Dorothy Wordsworth]

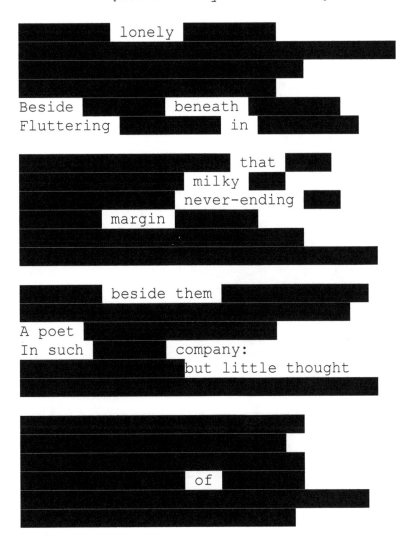

lonely

Beside beneath
Fluttering in

that
milky
never-ending
margin

beside them

A poet
In such company:
but little thought

of

The K

[For Women Who Are Not the Moon, tho not not-the-moon]

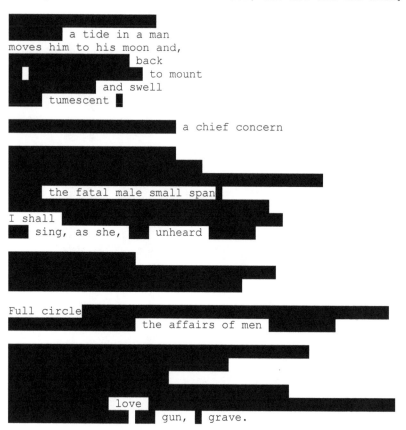

a tide in a man
moves him to his moon and,
back
to mount
and swell
tumescent

a chief concern

the fatal male small span
I shall
sing, as she, unheard

Full circle
the affairs of men

love
gun, grave.

These three poems are from an erasure series sourcing poems written by men who have variously erased the words, labor, and brilliance of the women who made those poems possible.

In the first two books of William Carlos Williams' epic five-book poem *Paterson*, published serially from 1946 – 1958, Williams inserts excerpts of letters written to him by the American poet Marcia Nardi. Published without her consent, Williams edited the letters and removed Nardi's name, attributing authorship to a fictional character named "C." The final five single-spaced prose pages of Book Two of *Paterson* is given over completely to Nardi's letters, in which she writes passionately and critically about the struggles of working-class women poets. In these pages of *Paterson*, the power of Nardi's letters overshadows Williams' tight literary project, as Nardi's expression of life overwhelms this celebrated book of US literary modernism. The irony of the letters' inclusion is sharp and confusing. Williams cedes the literary floor to her for a relatively large space of his book at the same time that he erases her authorship. Clearly, he recognizes Nardi's talent, the strength of her voice, and the truth of her words at the same time that he fails from his position of financial and cultural power to properly support and recognize her. I struggle with what to make of these contradictions.

I am both angry at Williams and grateful to him for including this writing that I otherwise would have never read—Williams' books were on multiple occasions put in my hands by professors and mentors; never Nardi's. Yet Nardi's articulation of how Williams consumes her life experience in the process of his literary production, as so many so-called male geniuses have done to the women they were supposed to have admired, was both the content and the form that was missing from the canon I was fed:

[late spring 1943]

My Dear Mr. P.

My feelings about you now are those of anger and indignation; and they enable me to tell you a lot of things straight from the shoulder, without my usual tongue tied round-aboutness.

You might as well take all your own literature and everyone else's and toss it into one of those big garbage trucks of the Sanitation Department, so long as the people with the top-cream minds and the "finer" sensibilities use those minds and sensibilities not to make themselves more humane human beings than the average person, but merely as a means of ducking all responsibility toward a better understanding of their fellow men, except theoretically—which doesn't mean a God-damned thing.

My attitude toward woman's wretched position in society and my ideas about all the changes necessary there, were interesting to you, weren't they, in so far as they made for literature? That my particular emotional orientation, in wrenching myself free from patterned standardized feminine feelings, enabled me to do some passably good work with poetry—all that was fine, wasn't it—something for you to sit up and take notice of! And you saw in one of my first letters to you (the one you had wanted to make us of, then, in the Introduction to your Paterson) an indication that my thoughts were to be taken seriously, because that too could be turned by you into literature, as something disconnected from life.

But when my actual personal life crept in, stamped all over with the very same attitudes and sensibilities and preoccupations that you found quite admirable as literature—that was an entirely different matter, wasn't it? No longer admirable, but, on the contrary, deplorable, annoying, stupid, or in some other way unpardonable; because those very ideas and feelings which make one a writer with some kind of new vision, are often the very same ones which, in living itself, make one clumsy, awkward, absurd, ungrateful, confidential where most people are reticent, and reticent where one should be confidential, and which cause one, all too often, to step on the toes of other people's sensitive egos as a result of one's stumbling earnestness or honesty carried too far. And that they are the very same ones—that's important, something to be remembered at all times, especially by writers like yourself who are so sheltered from life in the raw by the glass-walled condition of their own safe lives.

Only my writing (when I write) is myself: only that is the real me in any essential way. Not because I bring to literature and to life two different inconsistent sets of values, as you do. No, I don't do that; and I feel that when anyone does do it, literature is turned into just so much intellectual excrement fit for the same stinking hole as any other kind.

By publishing Nardi's letters without her consent and making it his own, Williams does exactly the thing Nardi accuses him of in this letter: he uses her experience as "literature," drawing a distinction between the two that in this case implicates genre and gender alike: the politics of literary recognition is gendered by genre. It is a familiar trope—the male genius takes the raw, chaotic material of a woman's writing and shapes it into a finely wrought form called *literature*.

For example, it is well known that William Wordsworth "borrowed" heavily from his sister Dorothy Wordsworth's journals to compose his poetry. Dorothy the diarist; William the poet. When I was in my early twenties, I began memorizing Wordsworth's poetry from a pocketbook *Selected* I pulled off my boyfriend's bookshelf. (The boyfriend was an aspiring novelist six years my senior who persuaded me to believe that the highest honor a woman writer could enjoy was to be her male partner's editor—a role to which he continuously attempted to recruit me by discouraging my own writing.)

Among other poems, "I Wandered Lonely as a Cloud," one of Wordsworth's best-known poems, became part of the inner landscape and rhythm of my literary imagination. In graduate school, when I began to write critically about Wordsworth, I read for the first time Dorothy Wordsworth's *Grasemere Journal*, first published in 1897, including this entry from which William Wordsworth's poem derives:

Thursday, 15th.[April, 1802]—It was a threatening, misty morning, but mild. We set off after dinner from Eusemere. Mrs. Clarkson went a short way with us, but turned back. The wind was furious, and we thought we must have returned. We first rested in the large boathouse, then under a furze bush opposite Mr. Clarkson's. Saw the plough going in the field. The wind seized our breath. The lake was rough. There was a boat by itself floating in the middle of the bay below Water Millock. We rested again in the Water Millock Lane. The hawthorns are black and green, the birches here and there greenish, but there is yet more of purple to be seen on the twigs. We got over into a field to avoid some cows—people working. A few primroses by the roadside—woodsorrel flower, the anemone, scentless violets, strawberries, and that starry, yellow flower which Mrs. C. calls pile wort. When we were in the woods beyond Gowbarrow Park we saw a few daffodils close to the water-side. We fancied that the sea had floated the seeds ashore, and that the little colony had so sprung up. But as we went along there were more and yet more; and at last, under the boughs of the trees, we saw that there was a long belt of them along the shore, about the breadth of a country turnpike road. I never saw daffodils so beautiful. They grew among the mossy stones about and above them; some rested their heads upon these stones, as on a pillow, for weariness; and the rest tossed and reeled and danced, and seemed as if they verily laughed with the wind, that blew upon them over the lake; they looked so gay, ever glancing, ever changing. This wind blew directly over the lake to them. There was here and there a little knot, and a few stragglers higher up; but they were so few as not to disturb the simplicity, unity, and life of that one busy highway. We rested again and again. The bays were stormy, and we heard the waves at different distances, and in the middle of the water, like the sea...All was cheerless and gloomy, so we faced the storm. At Dobson's I was very kindly treated by a young woman. The landlady looked sour, but it is her way...William was sitting by a good fire when I came downstairs. He soon made his way to the library, piled up in a corner of the window. He brought out a volume of Enfield's Speaker, another miscellany, and an odd volume of Congreve's plays. We had a glass of warm rum and water. We enjoyed ourselves, and wished for Mary. It rained and blew, when we went to bed.

William reproduces the images, words, and phrases of Dorothy's prose in his versified and rhymed rendition of her careful observation of this April morning. The scholarship on William and Dorothy's relationship suggests that the nature of this exchange was collaborative and consensual (though not all agree). But in terms of social and literary history, the results are uneven. What structures of social and literary hierarchies place a higher value on the poem over the journal? The same separation between literature and life that Nardi critiqued is reproduced in the history of the production, circulation, and reception of Dorothy and William Wordsworth's writing.

What is lost in this history? Whose voices are unheard or inaudible when *literature* categorically excludes the experiences and writing of women?

Returning to the 20th century US, one of the inheritors of William Carlos Williams' poetics, Charles Olson's poem "The K" (1949) expresses an entirely phallocentric and impoverished vision of the world in which women are agentless objects to be conquered or feared as all the world is to such an imagination. Predictably, Olson figures women as the exotic Eternal, unattainable Other, as Nature, as Moon. The unnamed woman "she" in his poem is "unheard" because he is incapable of hearing her song. At the same time, despite himself, Olson speaks a truth: We are the Moon and we do speak in voices that you cannot hear. Our poetry *is* our letters, journals, diaries, and songs. By contrast, your *literature* is only a sorry attempt to own and arrest the language of daily experience that we've already generously written down. But since your voice is, as always, the loudest, I've used your words to tell this story.

ADRA RAINE

CONTRIBUTOR BIOGRAPHIES

Ashely Adams is a swamp-adjacent writer whose work has appeared in *Paper Darts, Fourth River, Permafrost, Apex Magazine*, and other places. She is the nonfiction editor of the literary journal *Lammergeier*.

Amy Ash is the author of *The Open Mouth of the Vase*, winner of the 2013 Cider Press Review Book Award and the 2016 Etchings Press Whirling Prize post-publication award for poetry. Her work has been published in various journals and anthologies, including *Mid-American Review, Harpur Palate*, and *Salamander*. She is Assistant Professor of English and Director of Creative Writing at Indiana State University.

Making his home in Albany, New York, **Victorio Reyes Asili** is a PhD candidate at the University at Albany, working on his dissertation entitled *Mic Check—Finding Hip Hop's Place in the Literary Milieu*. He holds an MFA in Creative Writing and Poetry from The Vermont College of Fine Arts. Reyes Asili is also a regular panelist on hip hop, poetry, and other issues relating to craft and professionalization at the annual Association of Writers and Writing Programs Conference (AWP). His poems have appeared in many literary journals including *The Acentos Review, Word Riot, Pilgrimage Magazine*, and *Obsidian*, and his work has been anthologized in

Chorus: A Literary Mixtape, *It Was Written—Poetry Inspired by Hip Hop*, *Black Lives Have Always Mattered*, and *Boricua en la Luna: An Anthology of Puerto Rican Voices*. In addition to his work as a scholar and poet, Reyes Asili has been a lifelong activist and served as the executive director for the Social Justice Center of Albany for eleven years.

Andrea Avery is the author of *Sonata: A Memoir of Pain and the Piano* (Pegasus Books). Her work has also appeared in *Ploughshares*, *Real Simple*, *The Oxford American*, and *The Politics of Women's Bodies: Sexuality, Appearance, and Behavior*, 3rd Edition (Oxford University Press). She teaches in Phoenix, Arizona, and is at work on a novel.

Stacey Balkun is the author of *Eppur Si Muove*, *Jackalope-Girl Learns to Speak*, and *Lost City Museum*. Winner of the 2017 Women's National Book Association Poetry Prize, her work has appeared in *Best New Poets 2018*, *Crab Orchard Review*, *The Rumpus*, and other anthologies and journals. Chapbook Series Editor for Sundress Publications, Stacey holds an MFA from Fresno State and teaches poetry online at The Poetry Barn and The Loft. Visit her online at www.staceybalkun.com.

Iris Miriam Bloomfield is a writer, performance artist, and educator from Berkeley, California. She's just taking notes.

Chelsea Margaret Bodnar / 1990 / thrall to a wandering womb. Her poetry has appeared or is forthcoming in: *The Bennington Review*, *Rogue Agent*, *Sad Girl*

Review, Menacing Hedge, Thirteen Myna Birds, Wyvern Lit, and others. Her first chapbook, *Basement Gemini*, was published in 2018 by Hyacinth Girl Press.

Meghann Boltz is the author of the chapbook *rebel/blonde* (Bottlecap Press, 2018). Her work has appeared in *Cosmonauts Avenue*, *Peach Mag*, *Dream Pop*, *GlitterMob*, and elsewhere. She received her MA in Creative Writing from the University of East Anglia and was shortlisted for the 2018 Metatron Prize for Rising Authors.

Liz Bowen is a poet and critic living in New York. She is the author of *Sugarblood* (Metatron, 2017) and the chapbook *Compassion Fountain* (Hyacinth Girl Press, 2019). Her recent writing can be found in *The New Inquiry*, *American Poetry Review*, *Lit Hub*, *Boston Review*, *Cosmonauts Avenue*, *Dream Pop Journal*, *glitter-MOB*, *The Wanderer*, and elsewhere. She is a Ph.D. candidate in English and comparative literature at Columbia University, and a poetry editor for *Peach Mag*.

Tara Shea Burke is a queer poet and teacher from the Blue Ridge Mountains and Hampton Roads, Virginia. She's a writing instructor, editor, creative coach, and yoga teacher who has taught and lived in Virginia, New Mexico, and Colorado. She believes in community building, encouragement, and practice-based living, writing, teaching, and art. Find more about her work and www.tarasheaburke.com.

sally burnette is the author of the chapbooks *laughing plastic* (Broken Sleep Books) and *Special*

Ultimate: Baby's Story: a Documentary (Ghost City Press). Other erasures by them have been published in *petrichor*, *pidgeonholes*, *Poets Reading the News*, and elsewhere. They are originally from North Carolina but currently live in Boston, where they teach at Emerson College, work in a warehouse, and read flash fiction for *Split Lip Magazine*.

Tara Campbell (www.taracampbell.com) is a Kimbilio Fellow, a fiction editor at *Barrelhouse*, and an MFA candidate at American University. Prior publication credits include *SmokeLong Quarterly*, *Masters Review*, *Jellyfish Review*, *Booth*, and *Strange Horizons*. Her novel *TreeVolution* was published in 2016, followed in 2018 by her hybrid fiction/poetry collection *Circe's Bicycle*. Her third book, a short story collection called *Midnight at the Organporium*, was released by Aqueduct Press in 2019.

Zann Carter lives in Terre Haute, Indiana, where she hosts a monthly poetry reading now in its eleventh year. Her work has been published in *SageWoman*, *Witches & Pagans*, *Dream Pop Journal*, *Atlas and Alice*, and Driftwood Press. She twice won the Grand Prize in the Max Ehrmann Poetry Competition. Her website is: zanncarter.com.

Shane Jesse Christmass is the author of the novels, *Belfie Hell* (Inside The Castle, 2018), *Yeezus In Furs* (Dostoyevsky Wannabe, 2018), *Napalm Recipe: Volume One* (Dostoyevsky Wannabe, 2017), *Police Force As A Corrupt Breeze* (Dostoyevsky Wannabe,

2016), and *Acid Shottas* (The Ledatape Organisation, 2014). He was a member of the band Mattress Grave and is currently a member in Snake Milker. An archive of his writing/artwork/music can be found at www.shanejessechristmass.tumblr.com.

Caitlin Cowan is a writer, educator, and editor born and raised in the Midwest. Her poetry, fiction, and nonfiction have appeared or are forthcoming in *Pleiades, Gulf Coast, Tinderbox Poetry Journal, SmokeLong Quarterly, Entropy, The Dallas Observer*, and elsewhere. She has been the winner of the Littoral Press Poetry Prize, the *Mississippi Review* Prize, and an Avery Hopwood Award. Her poem "Flight Plan" won the *Fugue* Poetry Prize judged by Ilya Kaminsky. Her work has also received support from the Sewanee Writers' Conference and the Vermont Studio Center. She holds a PhD, MFA, and BA in English and Creative Writing, and has taught writing at a selection of institutions that includes the University of North Texas, Texas Woman's University, and Interlochen Center for the Arts. You can find her at caitlincowan.com.

For money, **Krista Cox** is a paralegal. For joy, she's managing editor of *Doubleback Review*, associate poetry editor at *Stirring: A Literary Collection*, and executive director of Lit Literary Collective, a nonprofit serving her local literary community. She's also an active member of the board of the Feminist Humanist Alliance. Her poetry has appeared in *Columbia Journal*, *Crab Fat Magazine*, *The Humanist*, and elsewhere. Find her at https://kristacox.me.

Formerly Laura E. Davis, **Laura Desiano** is the author of *Braiding the Storm* (Finishing Line, 2012). Her poems have appeared in *Tinderbox, Pedestal Magazine*, *Rogue Agent*, and *Voicemail Poems*, among others, and anthologized in *Bared* and *The Doll Collection*. Laura is a freelance writer in San Francisco, where she lives with her partner and son.

Caitlin M. Downs teaches creative writing, literature, and communications at the Pennsylvania College of Art & Design. She holds an MA in English from Arcadia University and is currently pursuing an MFA in Creative Writing at Wilkes University. Her visual poetry has been both published and exhibited, most recently in *Let the Record Show*—a collaboration with two other artists supported by the Pennsylvania Council on the Arts through Lancaster Public Art. She lives and writes in Lancaster, Pennsylvania.

Deborah Fass's poetry has been published in online and print journals including *Terrain.org*, *The Fourth River: Tributaries, New Directions*, *Kudzu House Quarterly*, *Lime Hawk,* and *The Clearing,* and in the anthology *Fire and Rain: Ecopoetry of California* (Scarlet Tanager Books). Her poetry chapbook, *Where the Current Catches,* won the 2017 Island Verse Poetry Prize from Island Verse Editions and was released in 2018. She holds an MFA in Creative Writing from Chatham University, where she received the Laurie Mansell Reich/Academy of American Poets Prize. She grew up in Los Angeles, went to Japan with a postgraduate Japanese Department of Education Research Fellowship (Literature), and now lives and teaches in the San Francisco Bay Area.

Caren Florance is a typographic artist and writer who currently lives and works in Canberra, Australia. Her recent practice-led doctorate explored the overlaps of visual poetry, text art, and artist books. She collaborated with poet Melinda Smith throughout her PhD, resulting in the limited-edition hand-printed book *1962: Be Spoken To* (2017) and its companion poetry volume *Members Only* (Recent Work Press, 2017). Their most recent collaboration was *Signs of Li*fe in the 2018 *Contour 556* public art biennial in Canberra. Her work is in national and international collections, mostly libraries. You can find out more at www.carenflorance.com.

Kegan Gaspar is a non-binary, queer poet and writer from Johannesburg, South Africa. Their writing seeks to narrate the complexities of being a queer body on the African continent, while also voicing the queerness that has been silenced and ignored throughout human history. They send you love and light!

Sarah Gerard's novel *True Love* is available from Harper Books (2020). Her essay collection *Sunshine State* was a *New York Times* Editors' Choice, and her novel *Binary Sta*r was a finalist for the *Los Angeles Times* Art Seidenbaum Award for First Fiction. Her short stories, essays, and interviews have appeared in *The New York Times*, *T Magazine*, *Granta*, and *McSweeney's*. Her collages have appeared in *Hazlitt*, *BOMB Magazine*, and *The Creative Independent*. *Recycle*, a co-authored book of collages and text, was published by Pacific in 2018. She is the 2018-19 New College of Florida Writer-in-Residence.

Callie Gill graduated with a BA in English Literature from The University of Texas at Arlington and an MFA from Texas State University. She currently lives in Dallas, Texas, with her partner and fat calico.

Tracy Gold is a writer, editor, and teacher living in Baltimore, Maryland. Her stories, essays, and poems have appeared in outlets including *YARN*, *Youth Imagination,* and *The Stonecoast Review.* Tracy teaches composition at The University of Baltimore, where she earned her MFA in Creative Writing and Publishing Arts. Tracy earned her BA in English from Duke University. When Tracy's not working, she's crawling on the floor with her baby, or hanging out with her rescue dog and horse. You can find out more about Tracy at tracycgold.com or by following her on Twitter @tracycgold.

Elisabeth Mehl Greene is a writer and composer working in the DC area. Her book, *Lady Midrash: Poems Reclaiming the Voices of Biblical Women*, was published in 2016 by Resource Publications, an imprint of Wipf and Stock. Recent work appears in the *Journal of Feminist Studies in Religion*, *Christian Feminism Today*, and the anthology *District Lines IV*.

Meg E. Griffitts is a poet and educator from Aurora, Colorado. She earned her MFA from Texas State University where she teaches. Her work has appeared in *White Stag*, *Crab Fat*, *Hypertrophic*, *BlazeVox*, and others. She collects succulents and cookbooks. More of her work can be found at megegriffitts.com.

Raye Hendrix is a poet from Alabama who loves cats, crystals, and classic rock. Raye received her BA and MA from Auburn University, and she is currently an MFA candidate at the University of Texas at Austin, where she was a finalist for both the 2018 Keene Prize for Literature and the 2018 Fania Kruger Fellowship in Writing, and where she serves as the Online Content and Web Editor for *Bat City Review*. Raye received honorable mentions for poetry in both *Southern Humanities Review*'s Witness Poetry Prize honoring Jake Adam York in 2014 and the AWP 2015 Intro Journals Project. Her work has appeared or is forthcoming in *Southern Indiana Review*, *The Chattahoochee Review*, *Shenandoah*, *The Pinch*, and elsewhere.

Joel Larson is an artist, writer, and performer from Libertyville, Illinois. Over-educated in liberal arts, he collaborated with an eclectic array of talents from Mickey Rooney to Tom Morello, wrote and produced for stage and television, and published his first e-book in 1999. Now, as a practicing puppeteer and letterpress printer, he is creating an intentional, creative, agrarian community in the "green belt" of Taos, New Mexico.

Katie Manning is the founding editor-in-chief of *Whale Road Review* and an associate professor of writing at Point Loma Nazarene University in San Diego. She is the author of *Tasty Other*, which won the 2016 Main Street Rag Poetry Book Award, and four chapbooks, including *The Gospel of the Bleeding Woman*. Her poems have appeared in *december*, *Glass*, *New Letters*, *Poet Lore*, *Stirring*, *Verse Daily*, and many other journals and anthologies. Find her online at www.katiemanningpoet.com.

Christopher "Rooster" Martinez is a writer and spoken word poet from SATX. He is earning an MA/MFA from the Creative Writing, Literature & Social Justice Program at Our Lady of the Lake University. He is the co-founder of the Blah Poetry Spot, a local poetry open mic and community organization. His work has appeared in such places as *Button Poetry*, *The Huffington Post Latino Voices*, *Pittsburgh Poetry Review*, *Pilgrimage Press*, the *Sagebrush Review*, and self-published chapbooks.

Kate Middleton is an Australian writer. She is the author of the poetry collections *Fire Season* (Giramondo, 2009), awarded the Western Australian Premier's Award for Poetry in 2009, and *Ephemeral Waters* (Giramondo, 2013), shortlisted for the NSW Premier's Award in 2014, and *Passage* (Giramondo, 2017). From September 2011–September 2012, she was the inaugural Sydney City Poet.

Ash Miranda is a nonbinary latinx poet and teacher from Chicago. Most of their work is an exploration of mental health, gender, and trauma. Their poetry collection *Thirteen Jars: How Xt'actani Learned to Speak* was published by Another New Calligraphy. They have a chapbook, *dolores in spanish is pain, dolores in lolita is a girl*, that focuses on sexual abuse and reclaiming Dolores Haze, published by Glass Poetry Press. Their work has been previously featured by *Yes, Poetry*, *Rising Phoenix Review*, *MAKE magazine*, and other publications. They tweet impulsive poetry and other musings @dustwhispers and you can learn more about their work at agirlaloof.com.

Rachel Anna Neff has written poetry since elementary school and has notebooks full of half-written novels. She earned her doctorate in Spanish literature and holds an MFA in poetry. Her work has been published in *JuxtaProse Magazine* and *Crab Fat Magazine*. Her poetry chapbook *The Haywire Heart and Other Musings on Love* was published by Finishing Line Press and her nonfiction book *Chasing Chickens: When Life after Higher Education Doesn't Go the Way You Planned* was published by University Press of Kansas.

Genevieve Pfeiffer facilitates workshops with survivors of sexual assault and harassment, and is the Assistant Director of Anomalous Press. Her work has been published in a few places including *Juked*, *So to Speak*, *Crack the Spine*, *Stone Canoe*, *BlazeVox*, and *The Write Room*. For someone who lives in New York City, she really enjoys climbing mountains. Genevieve was part of the 2019 AWP conference panel "Literary Sexual Abuse: From Silence to Safety." She's been the writer in residence at The Platte-Clove Preserve and The Mall of Found, and has done a few other things. You can learn about her project exploring herbal birth control's role in medieval Europe's witch trials and in colonization of the Americas, and the resulting influences on personal and bioregional health at: https://medium.com/@GenevieveJeanne.

Marcella Prokop is a writer, educator, and vagabond at heart. Neither wholly Colombian nor American, her dual identity shapes her writing and her place in the world. Marcella's work has been published online or in print by *Ploughshares*, *Pank*, *The Brooklyn Review*, and the *Christian Science Monitor*, among others. She is working on a collection of poems that explore social (in) justice in Colombia. Occasionally, she updates her blog at marcellaprokop.com.

Adra Raine, author of *Want-Catcher* (The Operating System, 2018), teaches literature and writing at the University of North Carolina at Chapel Hill where she is completing her dissertation, "Resonance Over Resolution: Resisting Definition in Susan Howe, Nathaniel Mackey, and Ed Roberson's Post-1968 Poetics." Meanwhile, she is currently at work on two manuscripts—*Wonder Weeks*, a document of the early years of parenthood, and *Undissertating*, which is what it sounds like it might be.

Sarah Lyn Rogers is a New York City-based writer from the San Francisco Bay Area, a contributing editor for *Catapult*, and the former fiction editor for *The Rumpus*. She is the author of *Inevitable What,* a poetry chapbook on magic and rituals. A collaborative poem Sarah wrote with Isobel O'Hare appears in the Black Lawrence Press anthology *They Said: A Multi-Genre Anthology of Contemporary Collaborative Writing*. For more of Sarah's work, visit sarahlynrogers.com.

Maggie Rosenau is a University of Colorado-Boulder PhD student with questionable prospects. Her projects concern texts and literary objects which feature no words. She uses methods of visual phenomenology to understand the aesthetic experience of reading nothing.

Ki Russell is author of the hybrid genre novel *The Wolf at the Door* (Ars Omnia Publishing, 2014), the poetry collection *Antler Woman Responds* (Paladin Contemporaries, 2014), and the chapbook *How to Become Baba Yaga* (Medulla Publishing, 2011). She is a peer reviewer for the online literary journal *Whale Road Review*. She teaches writing and literature at Blue Mountain Community College.

Elizabeth Schmuhl is a multidisciplinary artist—writer, dancer, painter—and the author of *Premonitions* (Wayne State University Press). She illustrates essays for *The Rumpus*, has taught writing at the University of Michigan, Ann Arbor, and worked in digital development at the Kennedy Center for Performing Arts. She is currently working as Shamel Pitts' Marketing and Campaign Manager. You can learn more at: @schmuhlface and elizabethschmuhl.com.

Jerrod Schwarz teaches creative writing at the University of Tampa and edits poetry for Driftwood Press. He has two chapbook collections *conjure* (Thirty West Publishing House) and *vaporware* (Plan B Press). His erasure poetry has appeared in *PANK*, *Entropy*, *Thimble Magazine*, *five;2;one*, and others. He lives in Tampa, Florida with his wife and twin toddlers.

kip shanks is a poet from New Jersey. they are starting the MFA program at the University of South Carolina this fall. their work can be found on VICE Motherboard. they can also be found on Instagram @kipshanks.

Australian poet **Melinda Smith** is the author of six books of poetry, most recently *Goodbye, Cruel* (Pitt St Poetry, 2017) and the poetry and art chapbook *Members Only* (Recent Work Press, 2017) with artist Caren Florance. She won the 2014 Australia Prime Minister's Literary Award for *Drag down to unlock or place an emergency call*. Her work has been widely anthologised and translated into multiple languages. She is based in Canberra and is a former poetry editor of *The Canberra Times*. She tweets as @MelindaLSmith and her FB author page is https://www.facebook.com/melindasmithpoet/.

Kitty Stryker is a feminist writer, anarchist activist, Juggalo anthropologist, and authority on developing a consent culture in alternative communities. She is the founder of ConsentCulture.com, a website that ran for six years as a hub for LGBT/kinky/poly folks looking for a sex critical approach to relationships. The site was relaunched in 2017 to support her book, *Ask: Building Consent Culture*, an anthology through Thorntree Press (2017). Kitty tours internationally speaking at universities and conferences about feminism, sex work, body positivity, queer politics, and more. She lives in Oakland, California, with her two cats, Foucault and Marquis. For media inquiries and bookings, email: miss.kitty.stryker@gmail.com.

Rachel Sucher

Addie Tsai is a queer nonbinary writer and artist who teaches courses in literature, creative writing, dance, and humanities at Houston Community College. She collaborated with Dominic Walsh Dance Theater on Victor Frankenstein and Camille Claudel, among others. Addie holds an MFA from Warren Wilson College and a PhD in Dance from Texas Woman's University. Her writing has been published in *Banango Street*, *The Offing*, *The Collagist*, *The Feminist Wire*, *Nat. Brut.*, and elsewhere. She is the Nonfiction Editor at *The Grief Diaries* and Senior Associate Editor in Poetry at *The Flexible Persona*. Her queer Asian young adult novel, *Dear Twin*, is available now from Metonymy Press.

Joanna C. Valente is a human who lives in Brooklyn, New York. They are the author of *Sirs & Madams* (Aldrich Press, 2014), *The Gods Are Dead* (Deadly Chaps Press, 2015), *Marys of the Sea* (Operating System, 2017), *Sexting Ghosts* (Unknown Press, 2018), *Xenos* (Agape Editions, 2016), and the editor of *A Shadow Map: Writing by Survivors of Sexual Assault* (CCM, 2017). They received their MFA in writing at Sarah Lawrence College. Joanna is the founder of *Yes, Poetry* and the managing editor for Civil Coping Mechanisms and *Luna Luna Magazine*. Some of their writing has appeared, or is forthcoming, in *Brooklyn Magazine*, *Prelude*, *BUST*, *Spork Press*, and elsewhere. Joanna also leads workshops at Brooklyn Poets. Follow at: joannavalente.com, @joannasaid, and @joannacvalente.

Jodi Versaw lives in Minneapolis, Minnesota. She works in education and believes in the importance of naming and breaking down heteropatriarchy and white supremacy.

Alex Vigue is a non-binary poet from Washington State. His chapbook *The Myth of Man* is available through Floating Bridge Press. He has recently had work appear in *Cotton Xenomorph*, *Gabby Journal*, and *Cahoodaloodaling*. You can find him on Twitter @Kingwithnoname or on his website at: alexvigue.wordpress.com.

Tyler Vile is a writer, performer, and organizer from Baltimore, Maryland, whose novel-in-verse, *Never Coming Home*, is available on Topside Press. She is a founding member of Hinenu: The Baltimore Justice Shtiebl, a radically inclusive synagogue. Her interactive poetry zine, *Hassidic Witch Murderer,* is available on her website (tylervile.wordpress.com). Her work has appeared in the Lambda Literary Award nominated anthology, *Resilience*, published by Heartspark Press, as well as the magazines *Femmescapes*, *Beltway Poetry Quarterly*, and *Rogue Agent*. She is currently working on her second collection of poetry and her first collection of speculative fiction.

Emily Walling's visual and written work can be found in *Apeiron Review*, *The Caribbean Writer, Cactus Heart*, *The MacGuffin*, a nuclear impact poetry anthology from Shabda Press, and other journals. She writes about the physical, emotional, and psychological connections people have with the natural world. She is a student in the

MA of Rhetoric and Writing program at the University of Findlay, and serves as the prose editor of *Slippery Elm Literary Journal.*

Logan K. Young's *1,000 Anagrams for La Monte Young* is out now via Peanut Gallery Press. A summer student of Thurston Moore at Naropa's Kerouac School, he's since been published everywhere from *Jacket2* to *3:AM* and anthologized as far flung as *An Anthology of Asemic Handwriting* (Uitgeverij) to the latest volume of the *Emergency Index* (Ugly Duckling Presse). Recent exhibitions include shows at Sediment Arts in Richmond, Virginia, and Labor in Mexico City.

Abigail Zimmer is the author of *girls their tongues* (Orange Monkey Press, 2017) and two chapbooks: *fearless as I seam* (Dancing Girl Press, 2014) and *child in a winter house brightening* (Tree Light Books, 2016), which received the 2016 Poetry Award from the *Chicago Review of Books*. She lives in Chicago where she is editor of the Lettered Streets Press.

EDITOR BIOGRAPHY

Isobel O'Hare is a poet and essayist who has authored three chapbooks as well as *all this can be yours* (University of Hell Press, 2018), a collection of erasure poems made from the apology statements of celebrities accused of sexual assault. O'Hare's work has appeared in numerous journals as well as the following anthologies: *A Shadow Map: An Anthology by Survivors of Sexual Assault* (Civil Coping Mechanisms Press), *They Said: A Multi-Genre Anthology of Contemporary Collaborative Writing* (Black Lawrence Press), and *Bettering American Poetry Vol. 3* (Bettering Books). They earned an MFA in Poetry from the Vermont College of Fine Arts and have received awards from Split This Rock and The Helene Wurlitzer Foundation of New Mexico. In addition to writing, O'Hare edits the journal and small press Dream Pop. They live in Taos, New Mexico.

ACKNOWLEDGMENTS

Thank you to every single contributor whose insights and talents have made this anthology what it is. Thanks also to Eve Connell, my editor at University of Hell, for her enthusiasm, encouragement, and guidance. Thank you to Greg Gerding for creating a safe space for this work.

SUGGESTED READING LIST

Abel, Jordan. *The Place of Scraps*. Talonbooks.

Adams, Sara. *Think Like a B*. SOd Press.

Flynn, Nick. *The Captain Asks for a Show of Hands*. Graywolf Press.

Foer, Jonathan Safran. *Tree of Codes*. Visual Editions.

Long Soldier, Layli. *Whereas*. Graywolf Press.

Macdonald, Travis. *The O Mission Repo*. Fact-Simile Editions.

Metres, Philip. *Sand Operas*. Alice James Books.

Nogues, Collier. *The Ground I Stand On Is Not My Ground*. Drunken Boat Media.

Philip, M. NourbeSe. *Zong!* Wesleyan University Press.

Reddy, Srikanth. *Voyager*. University of California Press.

Sharif, Solmaz. *Look*. Graywolf Press.

by **Leah Noble Davidson**
Poetic Scientifica
DOOR

by **Rory Douglas**
The Most Fun You'll Have at a Cage Fight

by **Brian S. Ellis**
American Dust Revisited
Often Go Awry

by **Greg Gerding**
The Burning Album of Lame
Venue Voyeurisms: Bars of San Diego
Loser Makes Good: Selected Poems 1994
Piss Artist: Selected Poems 1995-1999
The Idiot Parade: Selected Poems 2000-2005

by **Lauren Gilmore**
Outdancing the Universe

by **Rob Gray**
The Immaculate Collection / The Rhododendron and Camellia Year Book (1966)

by **Joseph Edwin Haeger**
Learn to Swim

by **Lindsey Kugler**
HERE.

by **Wryly T. McCutchen**
My Ugly & Other Love Snarls

by **Michael McLaughlin**
Countless Cinemas

by **Johnny No Bueno**
We Were Warriors
Concrete & Juniper

by **Isobel O'Hare**
all this can be yours (hardcover & paperback)

by **A.M. O'Malley**
Expecting Something Else

by **Stephen M. Park**
High & Dry
The Grass Is Greener

by **Christine Rice**
Swarm Theory

by **Thomas Lucky Richards**
Thirst for Beginners: Poems, Prose, and Quizzes

by **Liz Scott**
This Never Happened

by **Michael N. Thompson**
A Murder of Crows

by **Ellyn Touchette**
The Great Right-Here

by **Ran Walker**
Most of My Heroes Don't Appear on No Stamps

by **Sarah Xerta**
Nothing to Do with Me

edited by **Cam Awkward-Rich & Sam Sax**
The Dead Animal Handbook: An Anthology of Contemporary Poetry

edited by **Isobel O'Hare**
Erase the Patriarchy: An Anthology of Erasure Poetry

CPSIA information can be obtained
at www.ICGtesting.com
Printed in the USA
BVHW051543160820
586495BV00003B/23